BIDDLE'S
YOUNG
CARPENTER'S
ASSISTANT

BIDDLE'S YOUNG CARPENTER'S ASSISTANT

Owen Biddle

Introduction to the Dover Edition
by Bryan Clark Green

Dover Publications, Inc.
Mineola, New York

Bibliographical Note

This Dover edition, first published in 2006, is an unabridged republication (with slightly modernized spellings) of *The Young Carpenter's Assistant; or, A System of Architecture Adapted to the Style of Building in the United States,* originally published in 1805 by Benjamin Johnson, Philadelphia, and Ronalds & Loudon, New York. A new Introduction to the Dover Edition has been specially prepared by Bryan Clark Green.

Resetting the text for the Dover edition necessitated some slight departures from the original layout. Also, fold-out illustrations were reduced to fit onto one page or, in the case of Plate 41, one two-page spread. Minor errors and inconsistencies are from the original edition, and are retained here for the sake of authenticity.

International Standard Book Number

ISBN-13: 978-0-486-44736-0
ISBN-10: 0-486-44736-7

Manufactured in the United States by LSC Communications
44736702   2019
www.doverpublications.com

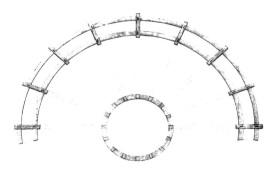

INTRODUCTION TO THE DOVER EDITION

BRYAN CLARK GREEN

Owen Biddle (1774–1806) lived a brief life, and his death at age thirty-two cut short a promising career at just the same time he was achieving a degree of renown. He left behind a handful of buildings, and one very important book upon which his reputation rests: *The Young Carpenter's Assistant; or, A System of Architecture, Adapted to the Style of Building in the United States.*[1] While the work advocates the Greek Revival mode of architecture, even more significant is the fact that it is the second architecture book produced in the United States, and the first written to teach the fundamentals of architecture and architectural drawing to the young craftsmen who were actively building the new structures so much in demand in the actively growing new nation.

Little is known about Biddle's life.[2] Born in 1774 to a Quaker clockmaker and member of the Philadelphia Monthly Meeting, Owen Biddle Jr. trained as a carpenter. He practiced his craft as a carpenter from 1799 to 1801 with fellow carpenter Joseph Cargill. Following that period, he was associated with Philadelphia's most prominent amateur architect, John Dorsey (1759–1821). Biddle executed, but did not design, the covering of the Schuykill Permanent Bridge (1798–1805), and built the Pennsylvania Academy (1805–06), designed by Dorsey.[3] A measure of the esteem which he commanded among his fellow craftsmen is evidenced by his election in 1800, at the age of twenty-six, to the Carpenter's Company of the City and County of Philadelphia. In 1803, Biddle designed the Arch Street Meeting House; his drawing for this project survives at the Athenaeum of Philadelphia (a second drawing of the same, attributed to Biddle, survives at Haverford College).[4] He was also in contact with Philadelphia's most important professional architect, Benjamin Henry Latrobe, who described Biddle posthumously in an 1807 letter as "a very good and honest man."[5] In *The Young Carpenter's Assistant*, Biddle described himself as "having been for some time past in the practice of teaching the rudiments of Architecture."[6] While it is assumed that Biddle learned his craft through the traditional means of apprenticeship, it is unclear where he learned to draw and design. His interest in architectural drawing and architecture books is notable, and is documented by the fact that he was a shareholder in the Library Company of Philadelphia. Biddle's inventory lists, in addition to his tools, "his paint

Figure 1. Arch Street Meeting House

box & mathematical instruments," and "15 books of Archititure [sic]."[7]

In addition to *The Young Carpenter's Assistant*, Biddle is remembered for two works completed during his brief career. The first, mentioned previously, was the Schuykill Permanent Bridge.[8] The bridge was destroyed by fire in 1875, but until that event, was a revered Philadelphia landmark. Biddle is best known for his design and construction of the Arch Street Meeting House (Figure 1, Arch Street Meeting House) that stands at Third and Arch streets in Philadelphia, and which he not only designed, but for which he also created a deft India-ink wash perspectival presentation drawing. He did

not, however, practice as an architect per se (Latrobe, a professional architect, acted as consultant on the Arch Street Meeting House design), nor did
he self-identify as one: as the identification on the title page to *The Young
Carpenter's Assistant* attests, Biddle perceived himself as a "House Carpenter
and Teacher of Architectural Drawing."[9]

The Young Carpenter's Assistant was the second architectural book written
and published in the United States[10]—preceded only by Asher Benjamin's
The Country Builder's Assistant (1797). The book is divided informally into six
sections. The first section (plates 1–6) focuses on the fundamentals of architecture and architectural drawing. Plates 1–3 involve the basics of architectural drawing, and plates 4–6 on drawing mouldings and cornices. The second section (plates 7–14) examines drawing the classical orders, beginning
with the Tuscan (plate 7), Doric (plate 8), Ionic (9–10), and Corinthian
(11–12). The Composite order is neither illustrated nor discussed. Plates 13
and 14 feature drawings comparing various mouldings and cornices. The
third section (plates 15–23) looks at discrete architectural details (occasional-
ly with suggestions for improving drawings of them). Details include variations on a frontispiece (plates 15–18), a dormer window (plate 19), mantel-
pieces (plates 21–22), and demonstration of proper incolumniation (plate 23).
The fourth section (plates 24–36) discusses construction details, including
roofs (plate 24), domes (plates 25–26), hipped roofs (plate 27), eaves (plate
28), centering for arches (plate 29), stairs (plates 30–31), handrails (plate 32),
elliptical stairs (plate 34), and gluing handrails in veneers (plate 35). The fifth
section (plates 36–40) contains student exercises for drawing plans and elevations. The sixth section (plates 41–44) features existing Philadelphia buildings, including the Schuykill Permanent Bridge (plate 41), Benjamin Henry
Latrobe's Bank of Pennsylvania, 1799 (plate 42), Samuel Blodget's Bank of the
United States, 1795 (plate 43), and the Steeple of Robert Smith's Christ
Church, 1755 (plate 44). The book concludes with a glossary.

Biddle clearly intended *The Young Carpenter's Assistant* to be used to
teach the basics of architecture and architectural drawing to young carpenters—like Biddle himself—who had no access to expensive architecture
books, or to books written specifically for American circumstances:

> Having been for some time past in the practice of teaching the rudiments
> of Architecture, I have experienced much inconvenience for want of suit-
> able books on the subject. All that have yet appeared have been written
> by foreign authors, who have adapted their examples and observations
> almost entirely to the style of building in their respective countries, which
> in many instances differs very materially from ours. Hence the American

student of Architecture has been taxed with the purchase of books, two thirds of the contents of which were, to him, unnecessary, when at the same time, in a large and expensive volume of this kind, he has not always been able to find the information he wanted."[11]

Biddle wondered that "Nothing on Architecture has heretofore appeared in this country."[12] "Why there has not," Biddle queried, "appears to me [a] matter of surprise, whilst we have among us men of talents, fully acquainted with the subject, some of which are also men of leisure."[13] "For my part," he rejoined, "I can conceive of few objects of more importance in a new and improving country like our own, as it regards our health and convenience, or as it may gratify the fancy, than the proper construction and building of our houses: whence I conclude it a matter of interest, not only meriting the attention of every carpenter, but of every man who has time and inclination to devote to the study, and more especially such who may have occasion to build."[14]

Biddle's particular focus was on the foundations of architecture, namely, the classical orders and the art of architectural drawing. On the subject of the orders, Biddle acknowledged his architectural debt to William Pain, from whom he drew them "with but little variation."[15] On the subject of geometry, and on the practicalities of constructing stairs and framing roofs, he looked to the many publications of Peter Nicholson, "whose works are held in most deserved estimation."[16] Biddle was also especially concerned with the art of architectural drawing—not surprising, from one who introduced himself on the title page as "House Carpenter and Teacher of Architectural Drawing."[17] "In choosing a case of mathematical instruments," Biddle recommended, "attention should be paid to its containing the scales of equal parts on the thin ivory or box rule, as in drawing the four Orders of Architecture, they are all proportioned by such a scale."[18] "The case," he continued, "should also contain a bow-pen or compass, a useful instrument for drawing black lead lines, a stick of Indian ink, two camel's hair pencils, one large, the other small, and a black lead pencil will constitute the instruments necessary in learning Architectural drawing."[19] India ink was essential: "It may be proper to observe that no kind of ink should be used except India Ink."[20]

Biddle was also concerned with the presentation of architectural drawing, especially in the subjects of shading (in elevation) and backlining (in plan). Shading was a technique essential to bringing out the detail of an architectural drawing. When constructing a drawing, Biddle observed, following the conventions espoused by Latrobe and other professional architects, "light should always come from the left side, and at an angle of forty-five degrees, both horizontally and vertically, by which the shadows of projecting moulding, &c. will always be equal to their projections."[21] To emphasize his point about the importance of shading, Biddle created a pair of plates, 16 and 17—an identical pair of pedimented door compositions—to emphasize the difference.

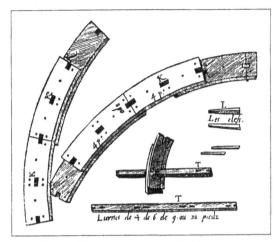

Figure 2. Delorme Dome, detail of rib lamination

Moving from elevation to plan, Biddle emphasized the importance of backlining, recommending that "in drawing the ground plan it will considerably enliven the drawing to give the appearance of a shadow on one side of the wall, by drawing one line thicker than the other; to do this he will suppose the light to come from the left hand upper corner of the drawing, and make the lines on the right hand and lower side of the walls and partitions thick, and the other sides thin lines."[22] Biddle included this feature in his plans; see, for example, plate 36, which accompanies the description above.

Biddle's sense of architectural propriety becomes clear, if not his sense of style: "In ornamenting a mantle [sic], the young carpenter would do well to endeavor at an imitation of something natural, and not to cover his work with unmeaning holes and cuttings of a gouge."[23] He continued: "Mantles [sic] and all other Architectural objects should always have a due proportion of plain surfaces, as a contrast to the ornamented parts."[24]

One of the most intriguing plates in Biddle's book is plate 26, "a Dome made with thin boards and small pieces of plank."[25] The plate records four accurate illustrations and an accurate written description of a simplified version of a light, inexpensive method of laminated plank rib construction promoted by Philibert Delorme (1514–1570), and published in 1561 in Paris in his *Nouvelle Inventions pour bien Bastir* (Figure 2). The most enthusiastic American proponent of this system was Thomas Jefferson; and it is probably through Jefferson's influence on Latrobe that knowledge of the Delorme dome reached Biddle. While in Paris, Thomas Jefferson was taken with the dome designed by Legrand and Molinos to cover the Halle au Blé (1782–83; later demolished), and the Delorme construction used for the dome. After discovering this system, Jefferson spent forty years promoting it, using it first

Figure 3. Pennsylvania Academy of Fine Art

at the second Monticello Rotunda at the University of Virginia, and later in his proposal for the President's House (1792), and the Hall of Representatives (1815). Jefferson, who owned a copy of Delorme's book, probably found the system attractive because it was inexpensive, required no centering, made use of wood—a material in ready supply in the United States, and brought dome construction within reach in America.[26] Under Jefferson's influence, the Delorme dome was employed by Robert Mills ("Building suited to a Public Officer" drawing, 1803; Circular Church, Charleston, 1804; Sansom Street Baptist Church, Philadelphia, 1808; Monumental Church, Richmond, 1812–17; Octagon Church, Philadelphia, 1813; Richmond City Hall, 1816, and First Baptist Church, Baltimore, 1816) and Latrobe (Navy Drydock proposal, 1803; the Hall of Representatives, 1805; the Roman Catholic cathedral in Baltimore, 1806–10 and 1817–21). Latrobe lectured at the American Philosophical Society on the Halle au Blé and acoustics in 1803, and was consulted on the design of the Arch Street Meeting House; so it is possible that it was Latrobe who first exposed Biddle to the Delorme dome.[27] Other American architects who employed the Delorme dome include Samuel Blodget (Design for the U.S. Capitol, 1792), Robert Cary Long, Sr. (Davidge Hall, University of Maryland, 1812), Maximilian Godefroy (Richmond City Hall, 1816; Unitarian Church, Baltimore, 1817), and Alexander Parris (Massachusetts General Hospital, 1823; Quincy Market, Boston, 1825).[28] Based on the profile of the dome, and Biddle's familiarity with the system, it is possible that the dome of the Pennsylvania Academy of Fine Art (Figure 3) was built using this system of laminated dome construction.

In plates 36–40, Biddle presents a selection intended as student exercises for drawing plans and elevations. Indeed, he describes his purpose: "In these plans it has been more my object to throw as great a variety into small compass as was readily practicable, than to give eligible plans for the builder, thereby aiming at instruction for the Student, which indeed has been my object throughout this work."[29] At least one carpenter-architect, a generation younger than Biddle, used *The Young Carpenter's Assistant* as just such a guide: Thomas R. Blackburn (1795–1867), of Virginia. Blackburn trained to become a carpenter, and after completing his apprenticeship, answered one of the many advertisements placed to attract young craftsmen to Charlottesville to erect Thomas Jefferson's University of Virginia.[30] While working at the University, Blackburn was taught to draw by Jefferson's master craftsmen John Neilson and James Dinsmore, and was loaned architecture books by Jefferson himself. While Jefferson's Palladio greatly influenced Blackburn's emergence as an architect in his own right, it was to *The Young Carpenter's Assistant* that Blackburn turned for more practical details. While such elements as stair construction and decoration were drawn in spirit from Biddle, Blackburn infused them with his own design sensibility just as Biddle intended.

Figure 4. Blackburn elevation based on Biddle

In one particular drawing, Blackburn drew on Biddle's plate 36, with a few minor variants.[31] He transformed Biddle's simple fanlight and narrow Doric porch into a more authoritative wide single-bay Tuscan portico, and surrounded the door with a larger fanlight and side-lights (Figure 4,

Blackburn elevation based on Biddle). Biddle's second-story window became a door topped by a top-light and surrounded by side-lights. Blackburn also dispensed with Biddle's Chinese lattice rail across the ridge of the roof, reduced it, and lowered it to the portico. It appears that Blackburn's design was built ca. 1842 in Augusta County, Virginia, for the Walker family (Figure 5, Walker House).[32] The only notable changes in the

Figure 5. Walker House

elevation as built were the transformation of the single windows into three-part windows (a typical Greek detail of the period, reflective of the increasing Greek influences on Blackburn's designs) and the loss of the original Tuscan porch columns. With the exception of stair details, which correspond to the scrolls drawn in the Blackburn collection, interior details are not recorded. These variations on a theme are exactly what Biddle intended when he wrote that it was his "object to throw as great a variety into small compass as was readily practicable . . . thereby aiming at instruction for the Student."[33] Departures from the plans and elevations presented were precisely the point, and this sort of architectural conversation was Biddle's intent.

The Young Carpenter's Assistant quickly proved to be popular. The first edition, published in 1805 in Philadelphia by Benjamin Johnson, went into wide circulation. Imprints of it found their way into the collections of Harvard University, the American Antiquarian Society, the New York Historical Society, Cooper Union, the Metropolitan Museum of Art, the Free Library of Philadelphia, the Carpenter's Company of the City and County of Philadelphia, the Library Company of Philadelphia, and the Library of Virginia.[34] Additional imprints of the first edition soon followed. Johnson and Warner, as the publisher became known, released a second imprint in 1810, which was "sold at [Johnson and Warner's] bookstores in Philadelphia, Richmond, Virginia, and Lexington, Kentucky."[35] The same firm also produced an 1815 imprint, which it sold from its bookstores in Philadelphia and Richmond. The next incarnation of the firm—Benjamin Warner—rereleased the edition in 1817, the final time the first edition would be available until this present reprint.[36]

   The Young Carpenter's Assistant returned to print twenty-six years later in 1833, with the second edition boasting a new introduction and twenty additional plates by the forty-one-year-old Philadelphia architect John Haviland. Published in the same year that Haviland began his restoration of the Assembly Room of Philadelphia's Hall, Biddle's work was retitled *An Improved Edition of Biddle's Young Carpenter's Assistant, being a Complete System of Architecture for Carpenters, Joiners, and Workmen in General, Adapted to the Style of Building in the United States.*[37] This edition proved to be nearly as durable as the first: McCarty and Davis would reissue it in 1837, and M. Pollock of Philadelphia would themselves release two imprints in 1854 and 1858.[38]

BRYAN CLARK GREEN
RICHMOND, VA.
JANUARY 2006

ENDNOTES

   1. Owen Biddle, *The Young Carpenter's Assistant; or, A System of Architecture, Adapted to the Style of Building in the United States* (Philadelphia: Benjamin Johnson, 1805).
   2. Excellent discussions of Biddle's role in Philadelphia architecture and the significance of *The Young Carpenter's Assistant* are found in Michael Lewis, "Owen Biddle and the Young Carpenter's Assistant," in *American Architects and Their Books to 1848*, eds. Kenneth Hafertepe and James F. O'Gorman (Amherst: University of Massachusetts Press, 2001), pp. 149–162; Jeffrey A. Cohen, "Building a Discipline: Early Institutional Settings for Architectural Education in Philadelphia, 1804–1890," *Journal of the Society of Architectural Historians* 53.2 (1994):

pp. 139–183; and Jeffrey A. Cohen, "Owen Biddle," in *Drawing Toward Building: Philadelphia Architectural Graphics, 1723–1986* (Philadelphia: University of Pennsylvania Press, 1986), pp. 48–50. Indispensable to the study of Philadelphia architecture is Sandra Tatman and Roger Moss, *Biographical Dictionary of Philadelphia Architects* (Boston: G. K. Hall, 1986); a biography of Owen Biddle is found on page 68.

3. Cohen, "John Dorsey," in *Drawing Toward Building*, pp. 39–41.

4. Ibid., pp. 48–50.

5. Benjamin Henry Latrobe to William Waln, 22 January 1807, in Thomas E. Jeffrey, ed., *The Papers of Benjamin Henry Latrobe*, Microfiche ed., Clifton, NJ, 1976, 54/F14, quoted in Cohen, "Owen Biddle," p. 50.

6. Biddle (1805), p. 3.

7. Will 1806:50, Philadelphia City Hall, quoted in Cohen, "Owen Biddle," in *Drawing Toward Building*, p. 49.

8. Biddle published a description of the bridge in the *Literary Magazine and American Register*, October, 1805, cited in Lewis, "Owen Biddle and the Young Carpenter's Assistant," p. 150. For an additional contemporary description, see Judge Richard Peters, *A Statistical Account of the Schuykill Permanent Bridge* (Philadelphia, 1807). For summary accounts of the bridge, see George B. Tatum, *Penn's Great Town: 250 Years of Philadelphia Architecture Illustrated in Prints and Drawings* (Philadelphia: University of Pennsylvania Press, 1961), p. 165, and Theo B. White, ed., *Philadelphia Architecture in the Nineteenth Century* (Second ed.; Philadelphia: The Art Alliance Press, 1973), p. 22.

9. Biddle (1805), title page.

10. Abraham Swan's *The British Architect* (London, 1745) was reprinted in Philadelphia in 1775, as was Swan's *Collection of Designs* (London, 1757), also reprinted in Philadelphia later in that same year. However, both of these books were reprints of architecture books written and originally published in England. See Bryan Clark Green, "Introduction," Abraham Swan, *A Collection of Designs in Architecture* (London, 1757); reprinted as *Georgian Architectural Designs and Details: The Classic 1757 Stylebook*. New York: Dover Publications, 2005.

11. Biddle, (1805), p. 3.

12. Ibid.

13. Ibid.

14. Ibid. Biddle's lament is not unlike that of Thomas Jefferson in his *Notes on the State of Virginia*, ed. William Peden. (1791. Reprint, 1955. New York: W.W. Norton, 1972). In 1814, Jefferson wrote his nephew Peter Carr, proposing special instruction for the "artificer or practical man." This included elementary and practical instruction, as well as a series of lectures, "given in the evening, so as not to interrupt the labors of the day." Thomas Jefferson to Peter Carr, September 7, 1814, Jefferson Papers, Special Collections, Alderman Library, University of Virginia.

15. Biddle (1805), p. 4. Biddle was probably drawing upon Pain's *Builder's Companion* (London, 1762).

16. Biddle (1805), p. 4. Here, Biddle was likely looking to Nicholson's *Principles of Architecture* (London, 1794–1809).

17. Biddle (1805), title page.

18. Ibid., p. 6.

19. Ibid.

20. Ibid.

21. Ibid., p. 23.

22. Ibid., p. 44.

23. Biddle (1805), p. 28.

24. Ibid.

25. Ibid., p. 32. Though he does not name it, Biddle has drawn and described a Delorme dome.

26. Douglas J. Harnsberger, " 'In Delorme's Manner ...': A Study of the Applications of Philibert Delorme's Dome Construction Method in Early 19th Century American Architecture," Master's Thesis, University of Virginia, School of Architecture, 1981; and Charles E. Brownell, Calder Loth, William M. S. Rasmussen, and Richard Guy Wilson, *The Making of Virginia Architecture* (Richmond: Virginia Museum of Fine Arts, 1992), pp. 51, 218, 220.

27. Ibid.

28. Ibid.

29. Biddle (1805), p. 48.

30. See Bryan Clark Green, "In the Shadow of Thomas Jefferson: The Architectural Career of Thomas R. Blackburn, with a Catalog of Architectural Drawings," Ph.D. Diss., University of Virginia, 2004. See also Bryan Clark Green, *In Jefferson's Shadow: The Architecture of Thomas R. Blackburn*. (New York: Princeton Architectural Press, forthcoming, 2006).

31. Thomas R. Blackburn Collection of Architectural Drawings, The Virginia Historical Society, Richmond, Volume I, front papers 9. See Green, "In the Shadow of Thomas Jefferson, pp. 114–115, 282. See also Green, *In Jefferson's Shadow*.

32. The Virginia Department of Historic Resources, Archives file 007–1068.

33. Biddle, (1805), p. 48.

34. Henry-Russell Hitchcock, *American Architectural Books: A List of Books, Portfolios, and Pamphlets on Architecture and Related Subjects Published in America Before 1895* (1946. Minneapolis: University of Minnesota Press, 1962), 16.

35. Owen Biddle, *The Young Carpenter's Assistant; Or, A System of Architecture Adapted to the Style of Building in the United States.* (Philadelphia: Johnson and Warner, 1810). While the title page does not indicate such, the volume is a reprint of the 1805 edition, and carries the copyright page from that first edition. The quotation about distribution comes from the title page of the 1810 imprint.

36. Biddle (1810), title page.

37. John Haviland, *An Improved Edition of Biddle's Young Carpenter's Assistant, being a Complete System of Architecture for Carpenters, Joiners, and Workmen in General, Adapted to the Style of Building in the United States* (Philadelphia: McCarty and Davis, 1833). See Matthew Baigell, "John Haviland in Pottsville," *Journal of the Society of Architectural Historians* 26.4 (December 1967), pp. 307–309.

38. Hitchcock, *American Architectural Books*, 16.

ILLUSTRATIONS

Figure 1. Arch Street Meeting House, Philadelphia. From Library of Congress, Prints and Photographs Division, Historic American Buildings Survey.

Figure 2. Delorme Dome, detail of rib lamination. From Philibert Delorme, *Nouvelle Inventions pour bien Bastir* (Paris, 1561). This illustration is taken from plate 14 of the 1576 edition, an edition owned by Thomas Jefferson.

Figure 3. Pennsylvania Academy of Fine Art, drawn by George Strickland, engraved by C. G. Childs, Philadelphia, 1828. Author.

Figure 4. House design based on plate 36 of Owen Biddle's *The Young Carpenter's Assistant.* From Thomas R. Blackburn Collection of Architectural Drawings, The Virginia Historical Society, Richmond, Volume I, front papers 9.

Figure 5. Walker House, Augusta County, Virginia (Photograph taken 1980s). From Virginia Department of Historic Resources, Archives File 007–1068.

BIBLIOGRAPHY

Baigell, Matthew. "John Haviland in Pottsville," *Journal of the Society of Architectural Historians* 26.4 (1967).

Benjamin, Asher. *The Country Builder's Assistant.* 1797. COMPLETE.

Biddle, Owen. *The Young Carpenter's Assistant; or, A System of Architecture, Adapted to the Style of Building in the United States.* Philadelphia: Benjamin Johnson, 1805.

Cohen, Jeffrey A. "Building a Discipline: Early Institutional Settings for Architectural Education in Philadelphia, 1804–1890," *Journal of the Society of Architectural Historians* 53.2 (1994).

Cohen, Jeffrey A. "Owen Biddle," in *Drawing Toward Building: Philadelphia Architectural Graphics, 1723–1986.* Philadelphia: University of Pennsylvania Press, 1986.

Cohen, Jeffrey A. "John Dorsey," in *Drawing Toward Building: Philadelphia Architectural Graphics, 1723–1986.* Philadelphia: University of Pennsylvania Press, 1986.

Hitchcock, Henry-Russell. *American Architectural Books: A List of Books, Portfolios, and Pamphlets on Architecture and Related Subjects Published in America Before 1895.* 1946. Minneapolis: University of Minnesota Press, 1962.

Lewis, Michael. "Owen Biddle and the Young Carpenter's Assistant." in *American Architects and Their Books to 1848*, eds. Kenneth Hafertepe and James F. O'Gorman (Amherst: University of Massachusetts Press, 2001).

O'Gorman, James F., Jeffrey A Cohen, George E. Thomas, and G. Holmes Perkins, *Drawing Toward Building: Philadelphia Architectural Graphics, 1723–1986*. Philadelphia: University of Pennsylvania Press, 1986.

Tatman, Sandra, and Roger Moss. *Biographical Dictionary of Philadelphia Architects*. Boston: G. K. Hall, 1986.

Tatum, George B. *Penn's Great Town: 250 Years of Philadelphia Architecture Illustrated in Prints and Drawings*. Philadelphia: University of Pennsylvania Press, 1961.

White, Theo B. *Philadelphia Architecture in the Nineteenth Century*. Second ed.; Philadelphia: The Art Alliance Press, 1973.

BRYAN CLARK GREEN is an Architectural Historian with Commonwealth Architects, an architecture and preservation firm in Richmond, Virginia. He is the author of a book about Thomas R. Blackburn, a carpenter who, while working for Thomas Jefferson at the University of Virginia, used available architecture books to begin his study of architecture. That work was published in 2005 as *In Jefferson's Shadow: The Architectural Career of Thomas R. Blackburn*. He was also co-author and co-curator of the book and exhibition, *Lost Virginia: Vanished Architecture of the Old Dominion*, which won the 2002 Gabriella Page Historic Preservation Award from the Association for the Preservation of Virginia Antiquities. Green received a B.A. from the University of Notre Dame, and an M.A. and Ph.D. from the University of Virginia.

BIDDLE'S
YOUNG
CARPENTER'S
ASSISTANT

PREFACE

HAVING been for some time past in the practice of teaching the rudiments of Architecture, I have experienced much inconvenience for want of suitable books on the subject. All that have yet appeared have been written by foreign authors, who have adapted their examples and observations almost entirely to the style of building in their respective countries, which in many instances differs very materially from ours. Hence the American student of Architecture has been taxed with the purchase of books, two thirds of the contents of which were, to him, unnecessary, when at the same time, in a large and expensive volume of this kind, he has not always been able to find the information he wanted.

Nothing on Architecture has heretofore appeared in this country, where the field for improvement in every useful art and science is, perhaps, more extensive than in any other. Why there has not, appears to me [a] matter of surprise, whilst we have among us men of talents, fully acquainted with the subject, some of whom are also men of leisure: perhaps they have not viewed the subject in the same light, or given to it the same degree of importance that I have. For my part, I can conceive of few objects of more consequence in a new and improving country like our own, as it regards our health or convenience, or as it may gratify the fancy, than the proper construction and building of our houses: whence I conclude it a matter of interest, not only meriting the attention of every carpenter, but of every man who has time and inclination to devote to the study, and more especially such who may have occasion to build.

Under the influence of these impressions, and at the solicitation of some of my friends, I have been induced to this undertaking. How far I have succeeded I leave to those who are capable of judging:—No doubt they will discover in it some imperfections, yet surely it will not be considered as arrogance in me to conclude it better adapted to the peculiar circumstances of this country than any foreign production of this kind. I have not, from prejudice, omitted any thing useful contained in the books already published on the subject—neither have I, on account of their authority, or from partiality, retained any thing I apprehended useless to the young Carpenter of the United States. The proportion of the four Orders I have taken from Pain's Works, with but little variation; and for some of the Geometrical problems I am indebted to Peter Nicholson, whose works are held in deserved estimation. In stairs and framing roofs I have given the most recent improvements of this country, and have endeavoured through the whole to adapt the explanations to the capacities of learners, which accounts for a minuteness that may possibly appear tedious to those who need no instruction.

PLATE 1

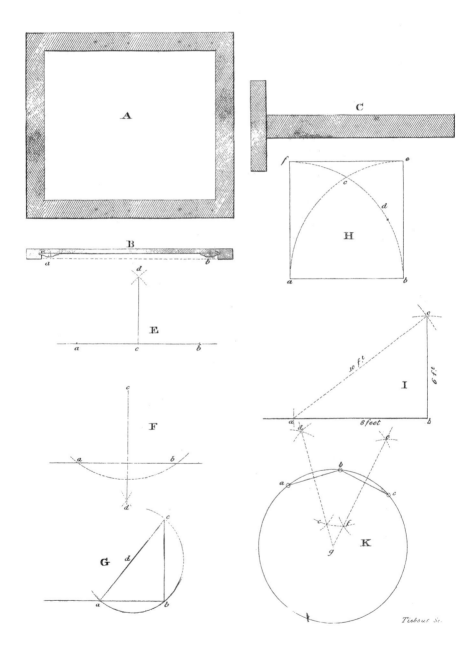

THE
YOUNG CARPENTER'S ASSISTANT.

As this work is intended for the student in Architecture it seems requisite to give some directions respecting the necessary instruments for drawing, &c.

Fig. A. Plate 1 is a representation of a draught-board, to which the paper used in drawing is to be fixed. This board is composed of a frame of mahogany or other hard wood (the outside edges of which should be exactly straight and square) with a pannel about half the thickness of the frame, to be let in from the back, and to lie in a rabbit in the frame, there to be secured by small wooden buttons. Fig. B is a section of the board, *a* and *b* are the buttons by which the pannel is kept in its place; eight or ten of these may be necessary. The pannel should be clamped, to remedy any disadvantage attending the shrinking of the wood. It would not be amiss before making the draught board to ascertain the size of the paper to be used, and make the pannel about 2 inches less each way than the sheet. In applying this board to use, lay the paper on a table, and moisten one side of it with a wet sponge, place the board upside down near it, take out the pannel and lay it on the paper, one inch of which will extend beyond the pannel all round, take hold by the edges of the paper and lift them both into the frame, fasten the buttons and dry the paper by the fire, when it will be smooth as a drum head.

Fig. C is the T square, the blade of which should be long enough to reach nearly across the draft board, and should not exceed three-sixteenths of an inch in thickness. Similar in form to this a bevel may be made, with the blade moveable on a centre in the stock. The application of these in drawing parallel lines on the draft board is so obvious that I need not describe it.

In choosing a case of mathematical instruments, attention should be paid to its containing the scales of equal parts on the thin ivory or box rule, as in drawing the four Orders of Architecture, they are all proportioned by such a scale; which indeed is the case with almost all Architecture drawings, and with a little attention the student will generally be able to find a scale ready made with greater accuracy than he would be able to make one himself. The case should also contain a bow-pen or compass, a useful instrument for drawing very small circles. With these, a small piece of gum elastic for rubbing out black lead lines, a stick of Indian ink, two camel's hair pencils, one large, the other small, and a black lead pencil will constitute the instruments necessary in learning Architectural drawing. It may be proper to observe that no kind of ink should be used except Indian Ink; for drawing lines this should be dissolved some time before it is to be used, but for shading it is best to drop a little water on a plate or saucer, and rub the stick of ink in it till it is of a proper shade.

I shall now proceed to explain some of the most useful geometrical problems, which every Carpenter ought to be acquainted with.

To raise a perpendicular or plumb line from a given point on a straight line:—
Let *a b* fig. E be the line, and *c* the point given, from which the perpendicular is to be drawn: take any space with the compasses at random, as *c b*; with that space set off *c a* and *c b*; then place one foot of the compasses in *a*, and extend the other beyond *c*, and describe a small part of a circle, as at *d*; then with the same extent of compasses place one foot in *b*, and make a part of a circle to cross the other at *d*; through the intersection of these circles a line drawn to *e* will be perpendicular or plumb.

From any given point over a right line to let fall a line which will be perpendicular to that right line:—

Let *c* fig. F be the point given; and *a b* the right line, with one foot of the compasses in *c* extend the other foot so as to describe the arc or part of a circle *a b*; place one foot of the compasses at the intersection of this arc with the right line at *b*, and extend them so as to describe a small arc at *d*; with the same extent of the compasses place one foot in the intersection at *a* and cross the arc at *d*; draw a line from *c* through the intersection of the arc at *d*, and it will be perpendicular to the right line at *b*.

On the end of a right line to draw a line which will be perpendicular or at right angles with that right line:—

Let *a b* fig. G be the right line; at some point over this line, as at *d,* place one foot of the compasses and extend the other to the end of the line at *b,* and describe the circle at *a b c* through the intersection at *a* and the center at *d,* draw the line *a d c,* from *c* draw the line *c b* which will be perpendicular to the line *a b.*

To describe a square whose sides shall all be equal to a given right line:—

Let *a b* fig. H be the line given; with one foot of the compasses on *a* describe the arc *f c b;* then with one foot in *b* describe *a c e,* divide the space *c b* into two parts at *d;* with the extent *c d* in the compasses set off *c f* and *c e;* connect *a f, f e* and *e b* and the square will be complete.

To lay off a square with a ten foot rod:—

Let *a b* fig. I be the given line; with eight feet of the rod from *b* make a mark at *a,* with six feet from *b* describe an arc at *c;* and with ten feet from *a* cross the arc at *c;* draw the line from the intersection at *c* to *b* and it will be square with the line *a b.*

Three points (not in a right line) or a small part of a circle being given to find a center which will describe a circle to pass through the point or complete the circle:—

Let *a b c* fig. K be the three points or part of a circle given; to find the center of which, place the foot of the compasses in *a* and describe an arc at *d* and *c,* with the same extent place one foot of the compasses in *b,* and cross the arcs of *d* and *c;* and at the same time describe arcs at *e* and *f,* then with the same extent of the compasses and one foot in *c* cross the arc at *e* and *f,* draw lines through the intersections of the arcs at *d* and *c* to *g,* and through the intersections *e* and *f* to *g,* the intersection of these lines at *g* is the center by which a circle may be drawn to pass through the points *a b c.*

To describe an Ellipsis mathematically to any given length and breadth:—

Let A C fig. A Plate 2 be the transverse, and B D the conjugate diameters; take half of B D and set it in from C to o; divide what remains from o to 3 into three equal parts; set one of these parts from o to *a*; make the distance from 3 to *b* equal to the distance from 3 to *a*, with the extent *a b* in the compasses describe the arcs *d b c* and *d a c*; these four points are the center by which the Ellipsis is drawn and the dotted lines passing through them and touching the Ellipsis mark how much of it is drawn by each center.

To describe an Ellipsis with a trammel:—
A B C D fig. B represents the trammel, being two strips crossing each other at right angles and halved together. In the middle of these strips is a grove; *a d* is the trammel rod on which are blocks made moveable like gauge heads, with a pin to each small enough to slide along the grove; at *d* is a pencil; fix the block or pin *c* so far from *d* as to be equal to half the conjugate diameter, and the block or pin *b* so far from *d* as to be equal to half the transverse diameter, place the pins in the grove of the trammel and on sliding them along the pencil at *d* will describe an Ellipsis.

An Ellipsis is being given to find the center and two axises thereof:—

Let A B C D fig. C be the Ellipsis; draw a line at random, as *a b*, through another part of the Ellipsis draw *d e* parallel to *a b*; through the middle of each of these draw *e f*, on the middle of which is the center of the Ellipsis, on which with an extent of the compasses of less than half the transverse and more than half the conjugate diameters, describe the circle intersecting the Ellipses in *g b i* and *k*; through the middle of *g b* and of *i k* draw the line A C which is the transverse diameter; bisect or divide this at right angles and it will give the conjugate diameter.

To describe a regular Polygon of any number of sides the length of one side being given:—

Let *a b* fig. D be the side given; on one end as *b* with any convenient radius or extent of compasses describe a semicircle; divide the round of this into as many parts as the polygon is to have sides, leave out two of these parts and with the length *a b* in the compasses set off from *b* to *c*, then from *c* to *d* then *d* to *e* when this is done place the compasses on *a* set off a *f*, then *f g*, connect *g* and *e*, and the Polygon is completed.

PLATE 2

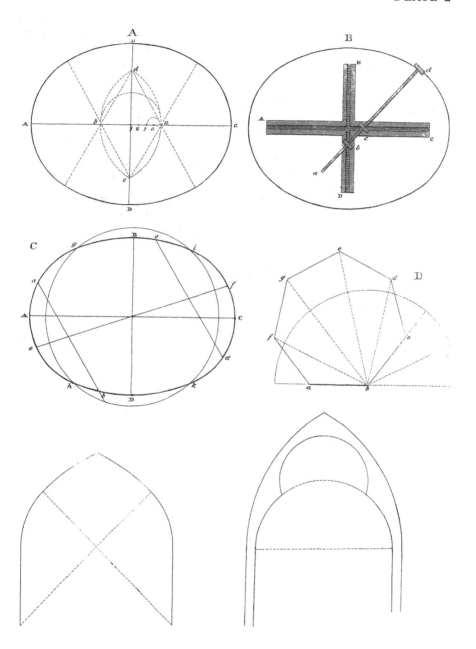

PLATE 3

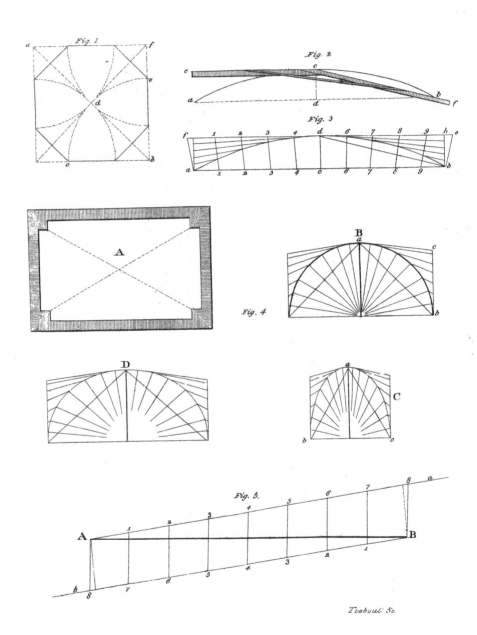

Fig. 1

Fig. 2

Fig. 3

Fig. 4

Fig. 5

Tiebout Sc.

PLATE 3

To describe an Octagon within a square, fig. 1:—

Draw the diagonal *a b*, and with the extent *b d* draw the arc *c d e*, then will *e f* be the quantity to lay off from each corner of the square, or if it is a piece of wood, to set the gauge for the quantity to be taken off from each corner.

To describe a segment of a circle of large radius with a trammel, fig. 2:—

Let *a b* be the chord, and *d c* the height of the segment; lay a strip with a straight edge from *b* to *c*, and then another from *c* to *e* parallel to *a b*, fasten them together and brace them with a lath, fix pins in the points *a c* and *b*, and slide the frame or trammel along these pins, and the angle of it will describe the segment required.

To draw a segment of a circle by intersecting lines, fig. 3:—

Let *a b* be the length or chord of the segment, and *c d* the height; draw the chord line *d b*, at right angles to which draw *b e*, through *d* and parallel to *a b*, draw *f d e*; divide *f e* and *a b* into any even number of parts, say 10, connect those divisions by the line 1 1, 2 2, 3 3, &c.; draw *b b* perpendicular to *a b*, and divide it into 5 parts; from the center *d* draw lines to these divisions, and where these lines cross the lines 1 1, 2 2, 3 3, &c., are the points through which to trace the segment.

To draw the arches of a groin, so that they shall intersect or mitre truly together, over a straight line, from a given arch of any form, fig. 4:—

A is the plan to be covered, B the arch of one side, which is here a semicircle, draw the chord line *a b,* which divide into any number of parts; from the centre draw lines through those parts, touching the arch, draw *b c* perpendicular to the base line, and from the crown of the arch at *a,* draw lines through the points of intersection of the former lines with the arch line, to the perpendicular line *b c*; lay off the width of one of the other arches as *b c* at C being the width of one end of the plan A, set up the height of the middle of the arch the same as B, draw the two chord lines *a b* and *a c,* divide them into the same number of parts as *a b* in B, transfer the perpendicular line *b c* from B to C, draw lines from the middle of the base through the divisions on the chord line, and from the top of the arch to the divisions on the perpendicular line, through the intersection of these lines the arch line required may be traced: D is the form of the groin or diagonal bracket traced in the same manner. This method may be applied to arches of any form, whether Elliptical, Circular or Gothick.

To divide a right line into any number of equal parts, fig. 5:—

Let A B be the right line given, to be divided into eight parts; from one end of it as at A, draw a line making an acute angle, as the line A *a,* from the other end of the line at B, draw another line parallel to A *a,* as B *b,* set off on these two lines, beginning at A and B, the number of divisions required, without regard to their turning out to the length of the line, as 1, 2, 3, 4, &c connect these by the lines 1 7, 2 6, &c. and where these lines cross the line A B is the point of division required.

PLATE 4

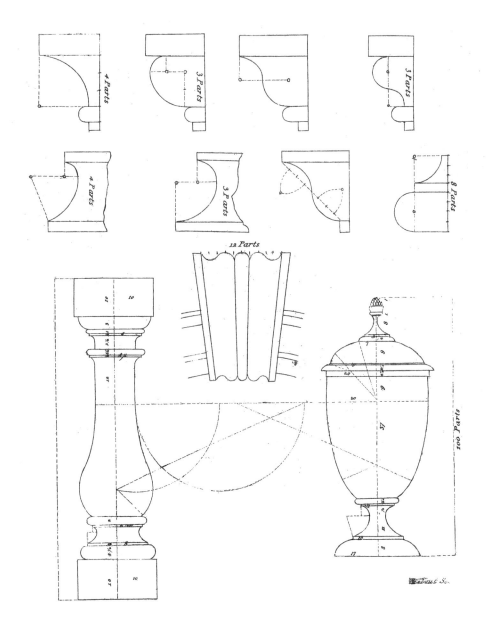

PLATE 4

REPRESENTS A FEW

MOULDINGS,

The centers for drawing which, being all represented, are perhaps sufficiently clear.

The Consol or Key should be in height equal to twice its width at bottom.

The Vase and Baluster are to show the manner of drawing compound circular lines, the meeting of the dotted lines showing the center. The student will observe, that when it is required to draw two or more circular lines of different radii, which are to appear smooth round, the two centers and the place of meeting of the different circles, should always be in a right line.

PLATE 5

Fig. A shows the method of enlarging a draft of a cornice; let the line *a b* be the height to which it is required to enlarge the cornice. Wherever this line crosses the different members of the draft mark it, and these marks will give the height of the different members of the enlarged cornice. To find the projection, enlarged in proportion: from the point *c* directly over the front of the wall draw the line *c d* at right angles or square with the line *a b*, on this line square over the projection of the different members of the draft, and that will give the projection required.

Fig. B is the method of contracting a draft. Let *a b* be equal to the height of the cornice required, from *b* draw the line *b c*, and where that crosses the different members of the draft, draw lines perpendicular to cross *a b*, which will be the height proportioned. To find the projection, contracted in proportion: from *c* draw the line *c d* at right angles or square with *b c*, then draw down the projection of the draught on this line, and from this line carry them square out to the line *d e*, which will be the projection contracted in proportion to *a b*. These two cornices with figures C and D, may serve as examples for the student to apply to frontispieces, &c. and the other three E, F and G are examples of Stucco cornice in the present fashion, of which G may serve where the story is low, and but little room over the window.

PLATE 5

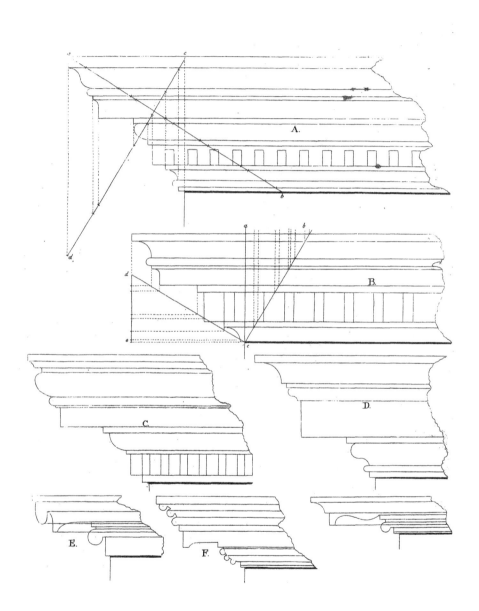

A.

B.

C.

D.

E.

F.

PLATE 6

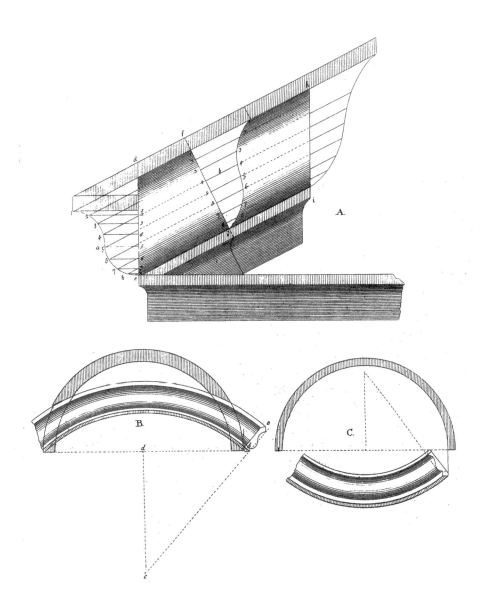

PLATE 6

Fig. A shows the manner of finding the form of a raking cornice, which will mitre with a level one; and the return at top for an open pediment. Let *a* be the level cornice; from the face of this, nearly at equal distances apart on the face, draw lines parallel to the rake, then draw the level lines 1 1, 2 2, &c, from the face of the cornice *a* to the perpendicular line *d e*; draw *f g* at *b* square with the rake, and make 1 1, 2 2, &c, at *b* equal to 1 1, 2 2, &c, at *a*; and trace the cornice through the points 1, 2, 3, 4, &c: which will be the form of the cornice required. The return at top is set off in the same manner from the perpendicular line *b i*, excepting that the projections at *a* are taken on the raking line.

Fig. B is the method of finding the sweep of a cornice which will bend round a circular wall and stand on a spring. Let *a* be a plan of the wall, *d* the center of it, and *b* the cornice drawn to its proper spring: draw the line *c e* touching the face of the cornice and continued till it intersects a line drawn perpendicular from the center *d*, the intersection at *c* will be the center from which to draw the cornice.

Fig. C is the method of drawing a cornice, to bend round the inside of a room, which being done by the same rule as the former, need no further explanation.

To Proportion the Four Orders of Architecture

THE TUSCAN ORDER.*

Plate 7

When this Order is to stand on a Pedestal, the whole height must be divided into five parts, one of which is the Pedestal, one fifth of the remainder is the Entablature, the other four fifths are the length of the Column including the Base and Capital: This divided into seven parts, one of them is the diameter of the Column just above its base; this diameter being divided into sixty parts or minutes, is the scale by which all the mouldings are proportioned, both in height and projection: a reference to fig. 1 will explain the proportions. Fig. 2 shows the proportion of the Mouldings, the heights, by the scale of 60 minutes, being set down on the outside lift marked at top with the letter H, and the projections measuring from the perpendicular line of the shaft of the Column, and the front of the Pedestal, in the other lift marked P. The Column in this Order is diminished to 45 minutes at its upper end.

*Of the TUSCAN there are no Examples of Antiquity remaining, excepting the Trajan and Antonine Columns at Rome, which are generally reckoned of this Order, being nearer in their proportions and mouldings to it, than to any other. It is supposed to receive its name from Tuscany, being more used there than elsewhere.

PLATE 7

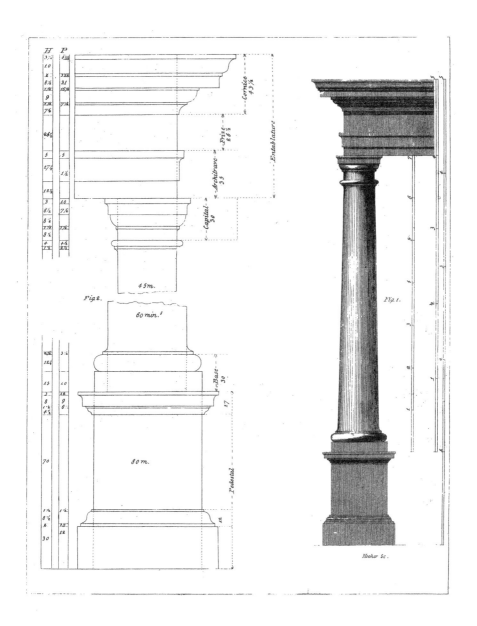

Fig.2.

45 m.

60 min.¹

80 m.

Fig.1.

Hooker Sc.

PLATE 8

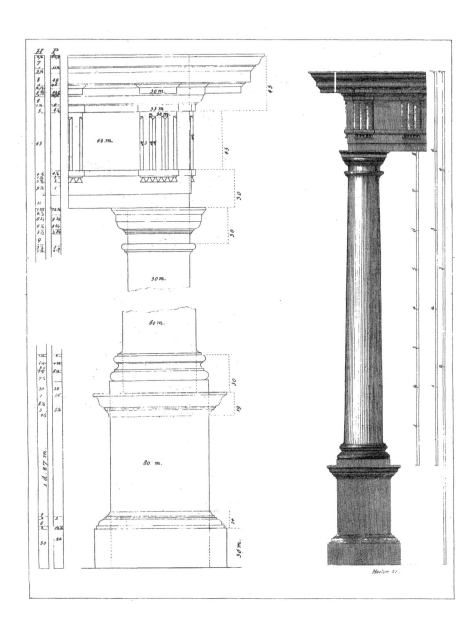

Hooker sc.

THE DORIC ORDER.*

PLATE 8

The general proportions of this Order are the same as the Tuscan, excepting that the diameter of the Column is one eighth of its length. The Column in this Order is diminished at its upper end to 50 minutes; the width of the trigliphs in the frize is 30 minutes; the distance from the middle of one trigliph to the middle of the next 75 minutes; this should be attended to in using this Order and those that follow, in Porticos, Collonades, &c; as a trigliph or modillion must always stand exactly over the middle of the Column. The distance between the centers of Modillions in this Order is so great, that the Columns cannot be coupled, as they frequently are in other Orders; the flutes of the trigliphs are 5 minutes wide each, and sunk 2½ minutes. The plancers and underside of the modillion are represented in Plate 13, and the method of drawing the scotia of the base is shown in Plate 10.

---

*DORIC, so called from Dorus, who, according to Vitruvius, built a Temple dedicated to Juno in the City of Argos, wherein the proportions of this Order were used, and which were afterwards adopted by the Cities of Achaia.

The Ornaments of this Order clearly evince it to have been the first invented of all the Orders of Architecture. In many instances the Columns are very short in proportion to their thickness, and without bases; and between the Triglyphs there is generally placed a bull's skull: the Architrave is sometimes made much wider than here represented, with only one facia, but I have preferred these proportions as handsomer.

THE IONIC ORDER.*

PLATE 9

One fifth of the whole height of this Order is given to the Pedestal; one sixth of the remainder is the Entablature, and the Column being divided into 9 parts, one of them is the diameter. The Column in this Order is diminished to 50 minutes at its upper end; the distance from center to center of the modillions is 31 minutes.

---

*Ionic from Ion the son of Xuthus, who, building a Temple to Diana, invented this Order. The Ancients generally made their Capitals in this Order flat, and to face only one way; but the angular Capital being thought by many more convenient, I have here given that.

PLATE 9

PLATE 10

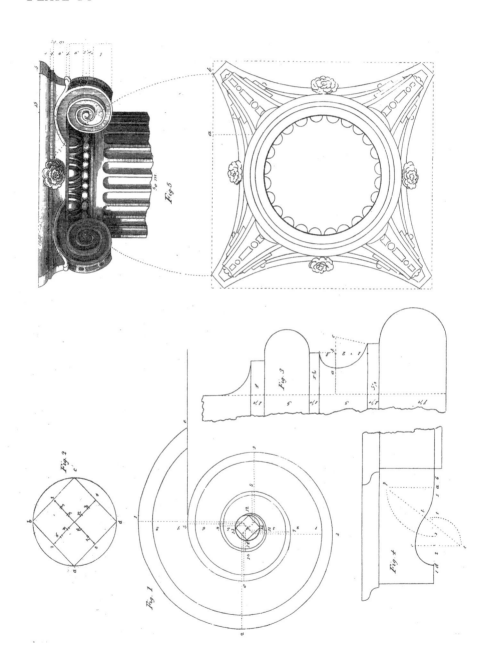

PLATE 10

To draw the Volute.

Divide the whole height of the volute, as in fig. 1, into 8 parts; in the fourth of these from the bottom draw a circle equal to one of those parts, within which make the square *a b c d,* which for a clearer explanation is transferred to fig. 2, on a larger scale, in the same position that the small one is in the volute; divide the square into 4 parts by the line 1 3 and 2 4, divide each of these lines into 6 parts, and number them as is there represented; to draw the volute, place one foot of the compasses on 1 in the eye of the volute, extend the other to 1 on the top of the volute, and draw round to 2 on the edge of the volute, then place the one foot on 2 in the square or eye, and draw the other round to 3, and so on taking each center in numerical order till it is all drawn; to find the center for the inside of the lift, set in from each center one fourth of the distance from that to the next one, as is represented in fig. 2; for the width of the lift at top take one sixteenth of the whole height, being 1½ minutes; to draw that part of the volute from 1 to 0, set the compasses at the bottom of the square.

Fig. 3 explains the manner of drawing the Scotia of the Attic Base; divide the height of the scotia into 3 parts, at the distance of one of these parts from the top draw the line *a b c,* on which *b* and *c* are the centers for drawing the scotia, and the line *a b c* is the limit of each quarter.

Fig. 4 is the Ionic Modillion, to draw which divide the bottom or projection into six parts, as 1, 2, 3, &c.: two and a half of these divisions up over *a* is the center of from *a* to *b*; under 2, one and a half divisions down, is the center of from *b* to *c*; and at 2 is the center of from *c* to *d*; the line *e f* from one center to the other marks the limits of each arc. Here I will take the liberty of remarking that when circles of different radii unite, and are required to appear smooth round, the two centers and place of meeting should always be on one line, as may appear in the two last examples.

Fig. 5 is the Ionic Capital on an enlarged scale, with a plan by which a clearer idea may be had of angular volutes.

THE CORINTHIAN ORDER.*

PLATE 11

The general proportions of this Order are, one fifth of the entire height for the Pedestal, one sixth of the remainder for the Entablature, and one tenth of the height of the Column is the diameter; the column diminishes to 50 minutes at its neck, the modillions are 11½ minutes wide, and 35 minutes from center to center of each, the dentils are 3½ minutes wide, and the space between each two thirds of a dentil. For an enlarged Capital and Modillion see next Plate.

*The following origin of the CORINTHIAN Order is given by Vitruvius:
"A marriageable young lady of Corinth fell ill and died; after the interment her nurse collected together sundry ornaments with which she used to be pleased; and putting them into a basket placed it near her tomb; and least it should be injured by the weather she covered it with a tile. It happened the basket was placed on the root of an acanthus, which in the Spring shot forth its leaves; these running up the sides of the basket, naturally formed a kind of Volute, in the turn given by the tile to the leaves. Happily Callimachus, a most ingenious sculptor, passing that way was struck with the beauty, elegance and novelty of the basket surrounded by the Acanthus leaves; and, according to this idea or example he afterwards made Columns for the Corinthians, ordaining the proportions such as constitute the Corinthian Order."
[*Rudiments of Ancient Architecture.*]

PLATE 11

PLATE 12

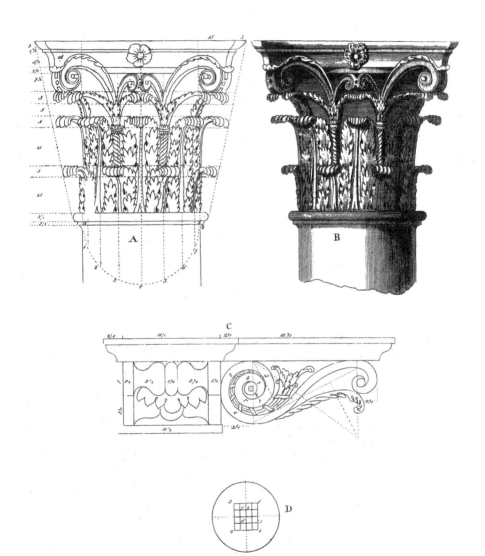

PLATE 12

Fig. A is the Corinthian Capital, the height being figured from the scale of minutes is plain to inspection; to find the place for each leaf, draw a semi-circle as *a 4 b,* equal to the diameter of the neck of the Column, divide the round of this into 8 parts, and from each of these draw lines through the Capital; these lines mark the place of each stock, or middle of each leaf. It may not be improper to remark that the inner break in the abacus or upper moulding of the Capital should not have as much projection as the outer one, as at *d;* if the real appearance of the moulding at *d* was given it would be very near a straight perpendicular line, but as that would not look well, a little liberty is taken to improve the appearance.

Fig. B is the same subject shaded, for the assistance of students.

Fig. C is the Corinthian Modillion, the parts being figured from the scale of minutes; fig. D is the eye of the Modillion on an enlarged scale; the centers are numbered, each center serving for one quarter of a circle, and these quarters are numbered in the Modillion.

PLATE 13

In this Plate is represented the Plancers of the Corinthian, Ionic and Doric Orders, at an external angle; the student may observe the Modillions in all cases correspond with the Column; and in the Doric Order they are enriched with drops, the shape of which is represented by the drops of the trigliphs.

PLATE 13

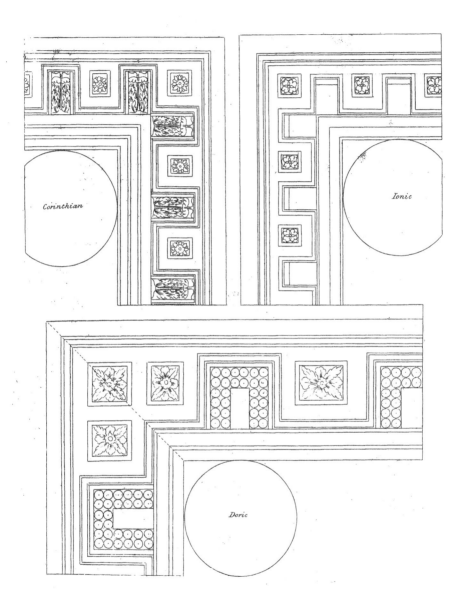

PLATE 14

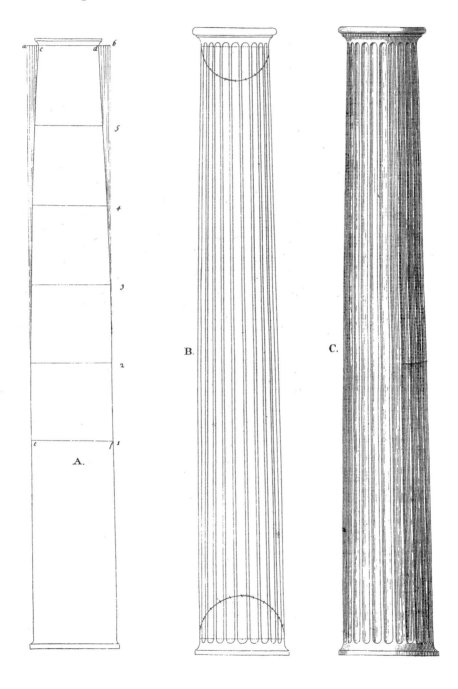

A.

B.

C.

PLATE 14

Of diminishing Columns.

Columns are sometimes diminished from the bottom, and sometimes the diminishing commences at one third of the height from the base. Fig. A represents a Column with the lower third part undiminished; divide the upper two-thirds into any number of equal parts, say 5, as at 1 2 3 4 5; *a b* at top is equal to the full thickness below, set in on each side from *a* and *b* half the difference between the size of the Column at top and that at bottom as *a c* and *b d*, divide each of these into the same number of parts that the upper two-thirds of the Column is; draw lines from *e* and *f* to each of those parts, and where these lines cross the divisions 1 2 3 and 4 will be the points through which to draw the edge of the Column.

When Columns are made of plank glued up the plank must each be diminished before glueing, in the same manner as if they were each a complete Column.

Fig. B is a representation of a Column fluted; draw a semicircle on each end of the Column; divide the round of this into 12 parts, and each of these again into 8 parts, 6 of these go to a flute and 2 to a fillet; observe that a flute will always be exactly in the middle of the Column.

Fig. C is a fluted Column, shaded, to show the effect.

Plate 15

In this Plate are given the lines of a pitch pediment frontispiece; in this the Column is made ten diameters in height; this is on a supposition that the door is for a town house with a narrow front, in which case the true proportion of the Orders may be dispensed with, and regard had to the general proportion of the building; but in country houses where the front may be well proportioned, the nearer we adhere to the Orders, the better will be the appearance in general. In fixing on the size of a door for the front of a house, it is better to make it rather too large than too small, as few things will make a house look meaner than a contracted front door; and where it will admit of it, the door should be as wide as half its height.

PLATE 15

2/9 of the Span

60 48 45 30

7 Parts

10 Diameters

7 Parts

50 m

9 Parts

8 Inches

Knapp fc.

SCALE

12 9 6 3 0   1   2   3   4   5

PLATE 16

O. Biddle del.   W. Knass sc.

PLATE 16

In this plate the foregoing subject is shaded. I will here observe that the light should always come from the left side, and at an angle of forty-five degrees, or on a mitre, both horizontally and vertically, by which the shadows of projecting moulding, &c. will be always equal to their projections; this will be better understood by examining the Plate.

As in geometrical drawings the relief or projection of the object can only be shown by the shading, the student should make it his business to understand the effects of light and shade; in those parts that stand forward, or project, the shade should be strong, and the part receiving the light should be bright, and as the distance increases both lights and shades should be weaker; all moulding, whether swelling or coving, will have both a stronger light and shade than plane surfaces exposed to an equal degree of light, and all surfaces on the same plane, not in a shadow, should have the same tint or degree of shade.

Plate 17

In this Plate is given a flat pediment frontispiece: the observations made on the preceding example with respect to general proportions, will apply to this.

After the student has fixed on the size of his door, he will draw the arch, and divide the half round of that into six parts, one of which is the width of the key at bottom, and two of them will be its height, which is also the top of the Columns; he may then find the diameter, and make a scale for proportioning the mouldings.

Plate 18

Is the foregoing shaded.

PLATE 17

SCALE

PLATE 18

O. Biddle delin.   W. Kneass sc

PLATE 19

Scale of Feet

PLATE 19

Is a Dormer window: the circular part of the sash is gothic; in drawing which the compasses should be kept at the same extent as in drawing the arch, and the center carried out on the top of the impost. If fluting or dentils are used for dormers, they should be larger in their proportions than in common work, and the pitch of the pediment may be rather steeper than in frontispieces, as the height will take off something from the pitch.

PLATE 20

Is a Venetian window in the Ionic Order. In giving a design for a window of this kind, the size of the glass should be made to correspond with the Entablature, so that it will be equal in height to one or two lights; and the sashes in the side window to range with the middle one.

PLATE 20

GENERAL OBSERVATIONS.

The four Orders of Architecture have been selected from such of the remains of ancient buildings as are supposed to be the most beautiful; and Paladio has been generally allowed to have been the best judge among the Moderns, who have given the proportions of the remains of Antiquity; the proportions in this book are pretty nearly the same as his; the differences are principally these:—There being no remains of Antiquity in the Tuscan Order with an Entablature, and Paladio having given a very poor one; succeeding Moderns have given that Order an Entablature near the proportion of the others, which I have adopted. The Doric Order has no example of a pedestal among the Ancients, and in the most admired building of Antiquity in that Order, the Columns have no base; and I believe there is no example remaining of the Ionic Order having modillions, but dentils only, though of late modillions have been as frequently applied as dentils. In the foregoing examples I have given to the Tuscan and Doric Order one-fifth of the height, exclusive of the Pedestal, for the Entablature; the Ionic and Corinthian each have one sixth; in situations where there are one or more Orders over another, this proportion in the upper should be altered; the richer Order always being uppermost, the Ionic and Corinthian may then have one-fifth for the Entablature. These proportions are all for small buildings, but if the buildings are large, exceeding 40 feet in height, the Entablature should increase proportionally; if one Order only is used, the Tuscan and Doric may have one fourth, Ionic and Corinthian one fifth; and if several Orders are used, the Ionic and Corinthian may have each one fourth of the height of the Order, exclusive of the Pedestal, for the height of the Entablature.

PLATES 21 & 22

Are four examples of Mantles. In ornamenting a mantle the young carpenter would do well to endeavour at an imitation of something natural, and not to cover his work with unmeaning holes and cuttings of a gouge.

Mantles and all other Architectural objects should always have a due proportion of plain surfaces, as a contrast to the ornamented parts. With strict propriety the faces of Architraves should never be fluted or carved: it very rarely occurs among the beautiful remains of antiquity, whose artists seem to have understood true taste much better than those of the present day, or their works would not have excited the admiration of so many ages. The use of composition ornaments on mantles, if judiciously chosen and placed, may have a very good effect, but care should be taken not to overload the work with them, and that there be a proper connection between the ornaments on different parts.

PLATE 21

PLATE 22

Tisort Sc

PLATE 23

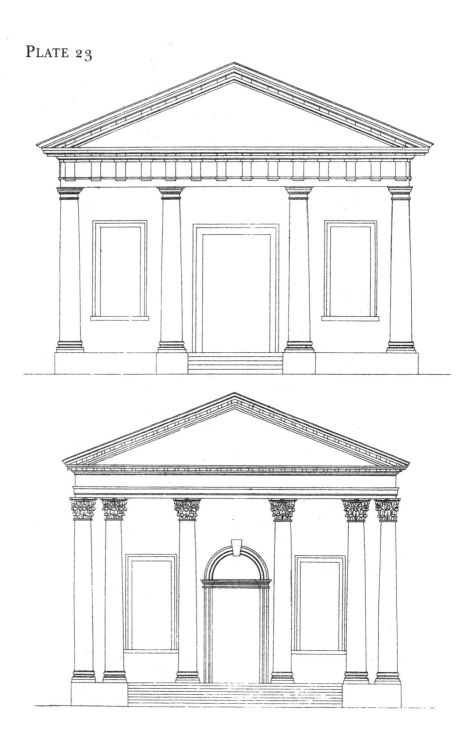

PLATE 23

Of Intercolumniation.

This plate represents two Porticos, one Doric and the other Corinthian; it is necessary in all Orders where there are modillions that the Column should be exactly under a modillion. The Doric order does not admit of the Columns being coupled, as they are in the Corinthian; the space from center to center of the modillions or trigliphs being but 75 minutes, when two columns with the bases touching would be 80 minutes from center to center. The examples in the Plate are both of small Porticos, and to admit of a convenient space between the Columns, the intercolumniation, or space between the Columns, is greater than it should be when the Porticos are large, and a graceful appearance is required; to admit of a free passage to the door the middle Columns are placed further apart than the others, though this is sometimes dispensed with, and the spaces made uniform.

PLATE 24

Of Roofs.

This plate gives three examples of framing for Principal rafters for roofs; in designing these, the material for the covering should be considered; whether it would require a strong frame and steep pitch, as tile or slate, or whether shingles, or any kind of metal is to be used.—Both the strength of framing, and the pitch of the examples in the plate, are calculated for shingles.

It is a considerable improvement in framing Principal rafters to keep them below the purlins, and to let the Jack-rafters lay on the purlins; the roof, besides being much stiffer, being easier regulated, or kept straight on the top; and the feet of the rafters are brought so far from the end of the girder as to be much stronger in their footing; the dotted lines at the foot of the rafter, show the shape of the tenon, which should be about half the thickness of the rafter, and the ends to fit hard in the mortise.—A screw-bolt to go through the girder up into the post, is a better way of supporting the girder than a strap; the nut is let into the post in the same manner that a bedstead screw is.

The customary pitch for roofs which are to be covered with shingles, is, one-third of the span for the height; and to find the length of the rafter take half the span and square it, and the whole height and square that, add the square of these two together, and from that sum extract the square root, which will be the length of the rafter.

Example.

Suppose a roof to span 45 feet, to rise one third, or 15 feet.

Half of 45 is 22.5		The height 15	
	22.5		15
	1125		75
	450		15
	450		
Square of half span	506.25	Square of the height	225

[continued p. 57]

PLATE 24

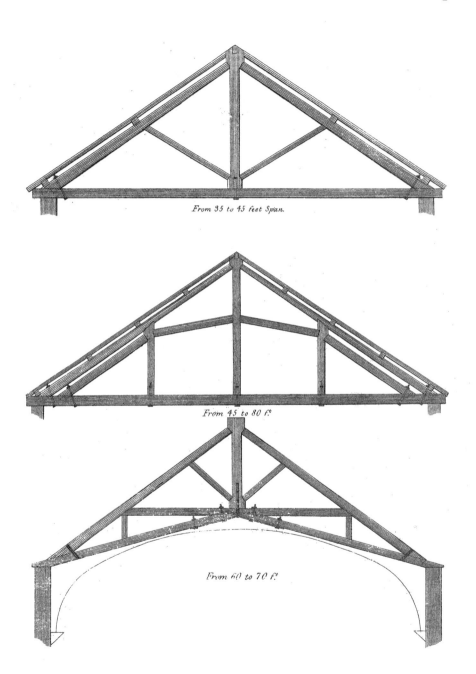

From 35 to 45 feet Span.

From 45 to 80 f.

From 60 to 70 f.

PLATE 25

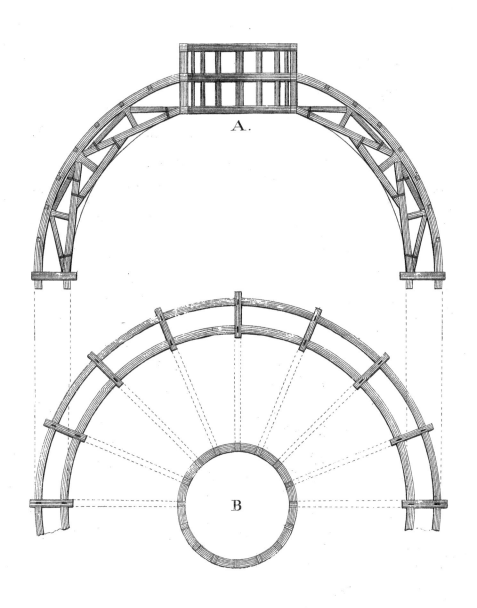

A.

B.

Square of half span 506.25
Square of the height 225.

                  .   .   .

            731.25 (27.0 feet, length of rafter)

            4

       47)331

         329

     540)225

PLATE 25

Of Domes.

A is the section and B is the half plan of the framing for a dome to have a vaulted ceiling and an opening for a sky-light; this frame is taken from P. Nicholson, and to me appears to be abundantly too strong; if we consider that the purlins form a number of bands round a roof of this form, which must burst before the roof falls in, we will find that we have little else to do but to connect the ends of the purlins so as to form hoops round the dome, and it is impossible for the roof to fall in while the hoops are entire.

PLATE 26

Dome of boards and plank.

Fig. A. is the section of a Dome made with thin boards and small pieces of plank; the principle of this form of roof consists in placing a number of hoops one above the other, and of such sizes as, when properly placed, will form the contour of the Dome; these hoops are here formed by pieces of plank, represented by fig. D at the bottom of the Plate; near each end of this is a pretty long mortise, the position of these is shown in the section A by *d d d*; fig. C is one of the ribs or rafters with a mortise in the middle of it long enough to receive two of fig. D, and at each end a sliding mortise of half that length, represented in section A by *c c c*; when these are to be put together, the wall plate (which should be of two thicknesses of boards, and made to break joint) should be first laid, and then a piece of the rafter, fig. C, should be fixed upright in its proper place and secured by a tenon at the lower end, which must go through the plate; it should be observed that the rafters are of two thicknesses, which should break joint, of course one of the first pieces should be but half the length of fig. C; when one set of the rafters are fixed all round, the pieces fig. D which form the hoops, or which I shall call the purlins, are fixed in them and secured by wooden keys which are driven, one on each side of the rafter through the mortise; by driving these keys more or less, the hoop may be lengthened or contracted, so as to bring it to the exact form or contour of the Dome, after the first set of purlins are fixed and properly keyed another set of rafters are placed, and then another set of purlins, until the Dome is complete.

The figure in the plate, for the sake of making its parts more clear, has been drawn considerably out of proportion, the materials being much too large, and a much greater number of purlins, would be proper. This principle of covering may be extended to a great span, and when the rafters come too close together at the top, every other one may be left out.

PLATE 26

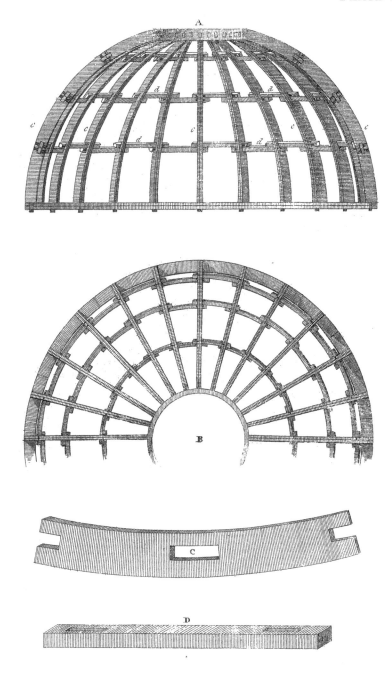

PLATE 27

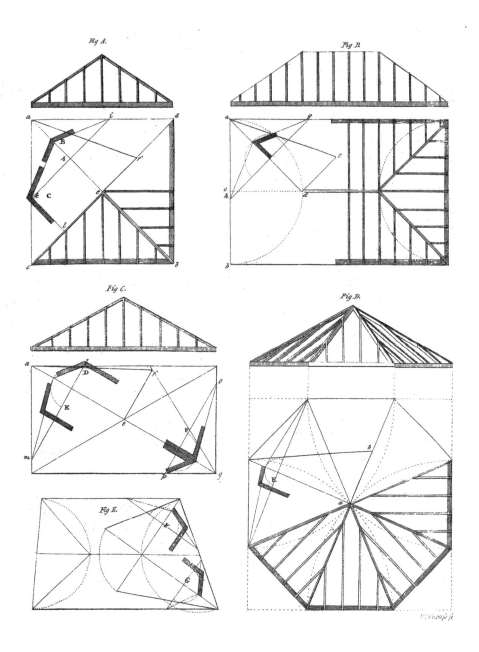

Fig A. Fig B. Fig C. Fig D. Fig E.

PLATE 27

Hip Roofs.

Fig. A is a square plan, to be covered with a Hip Roof; to find the length of the hip rafter, draw the diagonals *a b* & *c d* which will bisect each other at right angles at *e*; make *e f* equal to the height of the roof, and draw *a f* which will be the length of the hip rafter; to find the bevel of the back, draw *i k* at right angles with *a e* to cut it in any point as *b*, place one foot of the compasses in *b* and extend the other to the back of the rafter *a f* and describe a semicircle to cut the base line *a e* at *g*, then draw *g i* and *g k*, which will be the backing of the hip, as is shown by the level at B ; but the best way of working it is by the side bevel at C, which is made by drawing *l k* parallel to *a e*.

Fig. B is an oblong rectangular plan to be covered, with a ridge in the middle; make *c d* on the ridge equal to half the width *a b* and draw *a d*, at right angles to which make *d e* equal to the height of the roof, and draw *a e*, which will be the length of the hip rafters; as these may also answer for sky lights, and the hip rafters of those are sometimes mitred together, the bevel for the mitre is here given.

Fig. C is the same plan as the foregoing to be covered without any ridge; draw two diagonal lines to cross each other in the centre at *c*; draw *c f* equal to the height of the roof and at right angles with *a c*, and draw *a f* the hip rafter; to find the backing draw *m b* at right angles with *a c*, and proceed as in the former cases, when the two bevels D and E will be found by making their stocks parallel to the base line *a c*; at F is given the bevel for mitring hips for sky lights, found by drawing *o p* at right angles with the diagonal or base line.

Fig. D is an octangular plan; the hips are found in the same manner as the preceding, by making the height *a b* at right angles to one of the base lines, the bevel is shown at E.

Fig. E is the plan whose sides are parallel but the ends out of square; to find the hips, on each end as a diameter, draw a semicircle, and from the two centres draw the ridge, where the semicircles cross this will be the points to draw the base lines for the hips; the bevels F & G are found as before directed.

PLATE 28

In this plate is shown the manner of drawing the section of Eave; after the form of the cornice is fixed on, a section of it should be drawn either by a proper scale, or to its full size, and then the joist should be drawn with its lower edge on the plancere; from the top of the cornice draw the pitch of the roof, and from that set down the lath, rafters, &c: and it will show the proper place for the raising piece.

To proportion the Cornice to the height of the Building.

Divide the whole height into nineteen parts; one of these will be the height of the Cornice: this is a general rule, which may be varied to suit circumstances, as in a very high building, a steeple for instance, it would be too much; and in a very low one it would be rather too little; and as every thing is in some degree regulated by fashion, this should be attended to: the present fashion would be something smaller than the above proportion.

PLATE 28

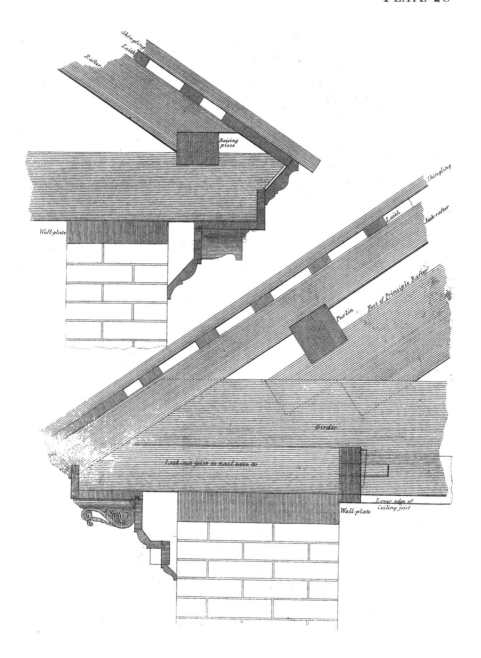

PLATE 29

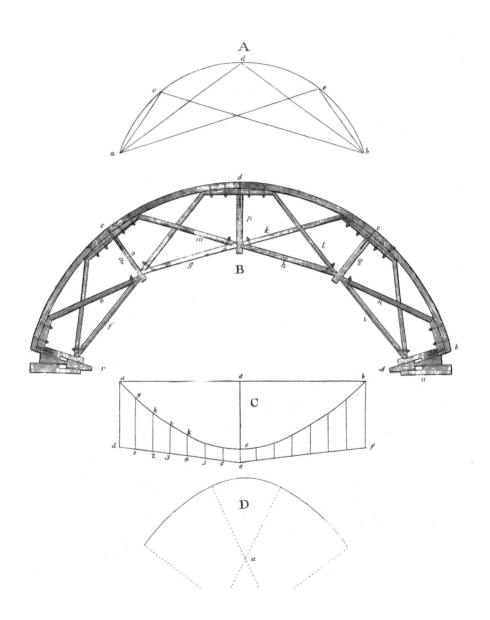

PLATE 29

Centres for Arches.

In making centres, the manner in which the framing is strained should be well understood, as frequently a piece of timber which is intended to form a tie, and framed to answer the end of one, will by an alteration of the pressure on the centre, in turning the arch, become a strut; and so vice versa, a strut become a tie; and joints which it was expected would be pressed hard, have become open, and required strapping to secure them.

Fig. A will explain a simple trussing for a centre; it is always expected that the abutments for the arch, are sufficient for the centre, and that a tie-beam across the bottom is useless, supposing the footing *a* and *b* are secure any two pieces of timber as *a c*, and *c b* connected at *c* like rafters, and footing at *a* and *b*, will bear any pressure at *c*, both acting as struts, and unless they bend the centre will not vary its shape at the point *c*; the same may be said of *a d* and *d b* and also of *a e* and *e b*.

It is on this principle the centre Fig. B is drawn, *a* and *b* being the abutments and *c d* and *e* corresponding with the same letters in fig. A, the pieces *f g b* and *i* are both ties and struts, and the joining of *k* and *l* into *b* should be made like the footing of rafters, as *b* is a tie for them while it forms a strut in a line with *m* and *n* to bear the pressure on the centre at *c*. In this frame the scantling is all short, if timber could be procured long enough to reach the length of the three pieces *m b* and *n*, it would be better to make it in one piece, and halve all the joints, the posts *o p* and *q* might then be in two thicknesses, and notched out to receive the frame between them, *r* and *s* are the striking wedges by which the centre is lowered after the arch is turned; *t* and *u* the blocking by which it is supported.

It is of considerable importance in making centres for large arches that the principle of equilibrium or balancing of arches should be understood: by this is meant that the line of the arch should be of such a curve, as to have no tendency in any part either to rise or fall; this curve is found by taking a chain of equal weight throughout, and suspending it from two points placed as far apart as the arch is to span, and allowed to sag till it touches a third point, placed equidistant from the others, and so far from a right line connecting them as the arch is to rise; the chain will then describe the true curve of an arch, which supposing the materials to be all equal in weight, will have no tendency to rise or fall in one part more than another; this is called the *Catenarian curve,* and is represented by fig. C, *a* and *b* being the points of suspension of the chain and the span of the arch, and *c d* the rise of the arch. It frequently happens that the arch is loaded more in one part than another, as in a bridge filling up over the haunches to level the road, to counterbalance this and preserve the equilibration of the arch, draw a section of the filling up, but with the drawing turned with the upper edge downwards as *d e f* fig. C; divide along this any number of equal parts as at 1, 2, 3, &c: and suspend to the chain *a c b* pieces of chain of the same make from the points *g b i k* &c. so as they may fall over the divisions 1 2 3 &c: these chains being cut so as to just reach the line of the road *d e f* will represent the filling in over the haunches and will make the chain *a c b* the form of an arch that will be equally balanced.

In fig. D, I have given a curve which will be pretty near the Caternarian, but drawn from centres with compasses, *a* is the center of the small part at top, and *b* and *c* the centres of the other parts.

PLATE 30

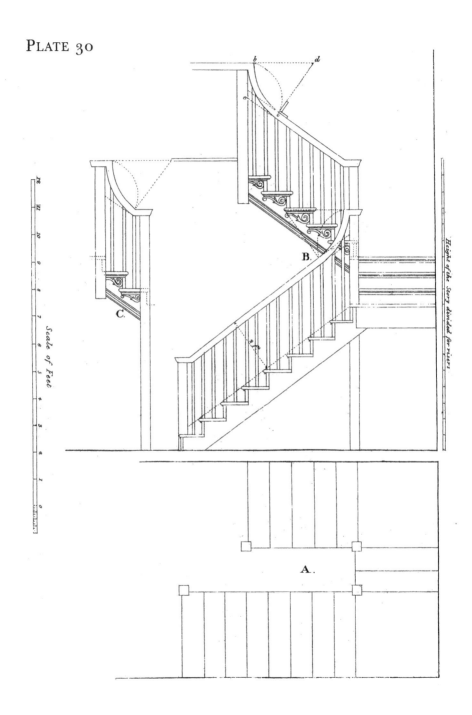

Scale of Feet

Height of the Story divided for risers

A.

B.

C.

PLATE 30

Of Stairs.

Fig. A is the plan of an open Newel Stairs, with two quarter-paces; and B is an elevation of the same, C being that part which is between the two quarter-paces.

To draw the Ramp of the Rail.

When a section of the steps is drawn, place the newel posts in their places, making them fair with the front edge of the steps, and draw the hand-rail, making it 2 feet from the top of the steps to the top of the rail; lay off the banisters, and let the mitre or knee of the rail come on the first banister; this gives the height of the first newel post; make the other posts all the same height, continue the line of the bottom of the rail up till it strikes the edge of the newel post at *a*, fig. B, place one foot of the compasses on *a* as a center, and extend the other to *b* at the top of the rail on the post and draw the arc *b c*; then draw *c d* square with the top of the rail until it meets the level of the rail on the post continued as *b d*, then will *d* be the center for sweeping the ramp.

PLATE 31

A is the plan, and B the section or elevation of a circular or geometrical stairs; in drawing the plan I have made the circular steps to come beyond the center of the circular part the width of one square step, by that means the ends of the circular steps are made wider and the difference in the rake of the handrail between the square and circular steps is not so great as it otherwise would be.

Fig. C shows the manner of drawing a bracket for the ends of the circular steps which shall correspond with one made for a square step; C is the square-step bracket; draw any number of parallel lines across this as 1 2 and those parallel to it, then from the point c draw $c\,d$ at any angle and equal in length to the circular bracket, draw ordinates from the lines in C as 2 3 and those parallel to it, touching the line $c\,d$; continue those lines at right angles with $c\,d$ as 3, 4, and those parallel to it; take the distance of the ordinates from the line $e\,c$ to the edges of the bracket C and mark them on the corresponding line in the short bracket from the line $d\,c$ and through those points trace the form of the circular bracket.

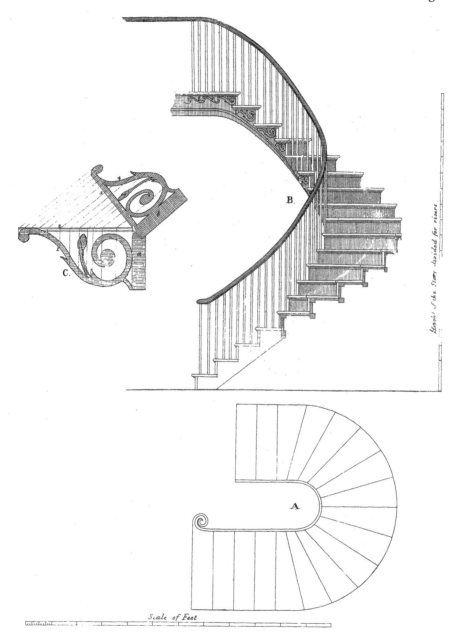

PLATE 31

B.

C.

A

Scale of Feet

Height of the Story divided for risers

PLATE 32

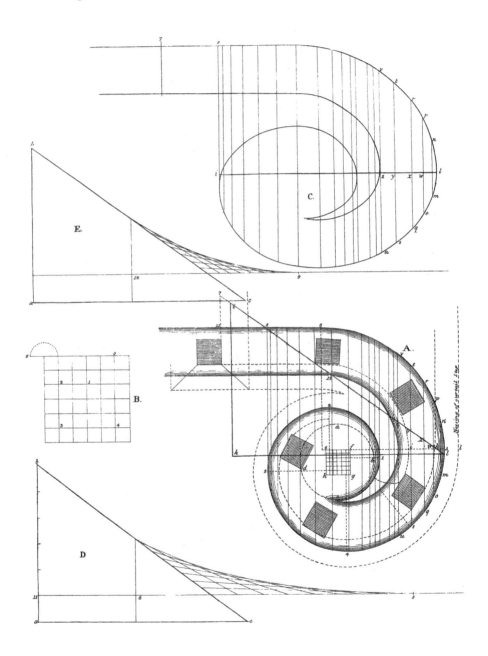

PLATE 32

To draw the Scroll for a Hand-rail.

Make a circle three inches and an half diameter, as *a b c d* fig. A; within this make a square equal to one third the diameter of the circle, as *e f g b,* divide this into 36 small squares as is represented in fig. B on its full size, and laid in the same position as in A, and with the centres numbered by which the scroll is drawn, place one foot of the compasses on 1 in the square, and extend them to *c* and draw round to 1 on the edge of the rail, then set the compasses in 2 in the square and extending them to 1 draw round to 2 on the edge, and so on till the whole is drawn round to 6; to draw the outside of the rail, set in its thickness from 6 to 12, and go back by the same numbers and the scroll will be complete.

To draw the curtail step.

At *i k* in fig. A place the thickness of a banister, and set out to *l* the projection of the nosing, with the same centres used for drawing the scroll, draw this round till it meets the nosing at the end of the step drawn with the same projection; the thickness of the banisters being set off may be drawn round in the scroll and they may be spaced off, making them the same distance apart that the other banisters are.

To draw the Face Mould.

Draw the pitch board *i k l* fig. A, making the base *k l* cut the scroll as near its centre or widest part as possible; draw ordinates or parallel lines as *m n, o p, q r,* &c. across the scroll; draw the line *i l* in fig. C, and make the spaces *l w x y* &c. in fig. C agree with the spaces *l w x y* &c. on the line *l i* in fig. A; draw lines through those points in fig. C at right angles with *i l* as *m n o p,* &c. take the distances from the line *k l* to the edge of the scroll at A, and transfer them to C, as *m n, o p* &c. taking to the edge of the rail both inside and outside; through these points the face mould C may be traced with a steady hand; continue the line of the pitch board in A up till it strikes the riser of the second step, as from 8 to 7 and set that space off at C from 8 to 7, at which place square over a strong mark, the use of which will be explained hereafter.

To draw the Falling Mould.

Draw the pitch board at D, take off one sixth from the bottom and draw the line 11 6 *s* take the distance from 11 to 6 in A, and set it from 11 to 6 in D, make the distance from 6 to *s* in D equal to the distances round the rail from 6 to *s* in A (being any distance beyond the first quarter,) by tracing round with a small space in the compasses; divide the rake of the rail on the pitch board and the level of it out to *s* into any equal number of parts and by drawing intersecting lines the top of the rail is given.

The falling mould for the outside is drawn in the same manner, excepting the distance from 12 to 9 is taken from the outside of the rail from 12 to 9, fig. A.

In applying these to use, the mark at 7 on C should be made to correspond with the edge *a b* of the pitch board in the falling moulds D and E.

PLATE 33

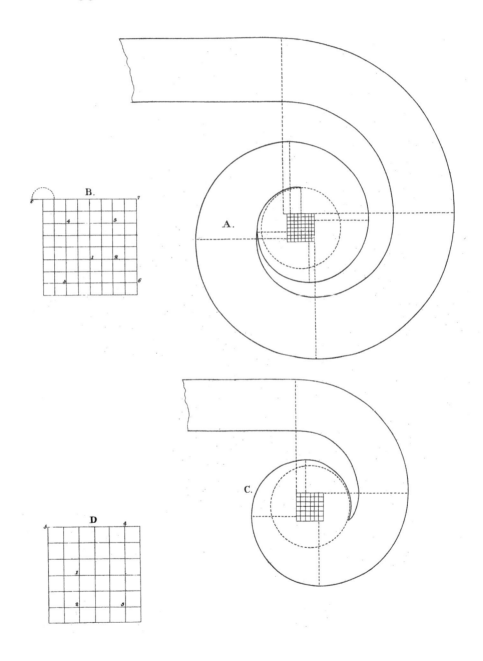

PLATE 33

In this Plate is given two more examples of scrolls of different sizes, B and D contains the centres for drawing, both figured. It may be well here to observe, that in drawing the scroll, a line should be drawn from the center about to be used through the one used last, out to the edge of the scroll; this shows where to commence the sweep for that quarter; the dotted lines in A and C will make this clearer.

78 OWEN BIDDLE

PLATE 34

To draw the Moulds for an Elliptical Stairs.

The plan of the rail being drawn, and the ends of the steps being all of equal width on the rail, it should be divided round into as many equal parts as there are steps, then take the tread of any number of steps, suppose 8, and let *b b* fig. H be the tread of 8 steps, on the perpendicular *b m* set up the height of 8 risers, and draw the line *m b* which will be the under edge of the falling mould; the Student will observe, that this falling mould will be a straight line excepting a little turn at the landing; next mark the plan of the rail into as many parts as there are to be pieces in the rail (in this there are three), then draw a chord line to the joints, as at E C and G; also draw lines parallel to the chords to touch the convex sides of the rail as *b b,* from every joint draw perpendiculars to their respective chords; now the tread of the middle piece at C being just 8 steps, and the section H being for the same number, set up *b m n* in B equal to *b m n* in H, and make *i b* in B equal in height to *i b* in H; then draw *n i* and draw the ordinates 1 *a,* 1 2 *b* , 1 3 *c,* &c. continued till they touch the line *n i*; prick off the ordinates on the face mould from the plan C agreeable to the figuring, and trace the mould through those points, and it will be complete.

The moulds for D, and F, being only for 6 steps each, the tread of 6 steps should be set off from *b* to H in fig. H, and the height H *k l* set up from the chord lines at D and F; as for the rest it is the same as B.

PLATE 34

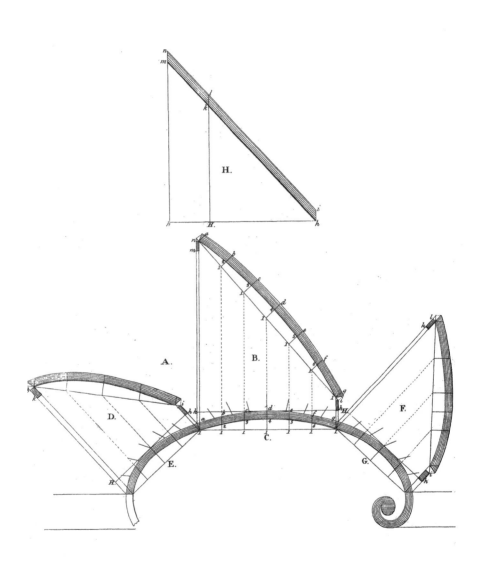

PLATE 35

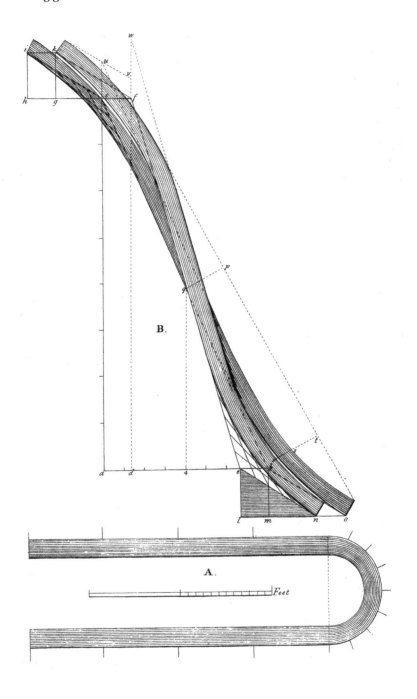

B.

A.

Feet

PLATE 35

To draw the Moulds for gluing Hand-rails in Veneers.

Draw a plan of the rail, as A, on which mark the steps; the twisted part of the rail which is to be veneered, should reach over one of the square steps, both at top and bottom; make *a b* in fig. B equal to stretch out of the outside or greatest circle in fig. A. and *a c* equal to the height of the risers, again *d e* is the compass of the lesser circle, set in the middle between *a* and *b*; and *d f* is the height of the steps the same as before, therefore the triangle *a b c* is the pitch board for the inside falling mould, and *b m o* at bottom and *i b c* at top are the pitch boards of two common steps; which lines when intersected will give the under line of the inside falling mould. In the same manner *d f e*, with the two common steps *k g f* at the top and *e l n* at the bottom will give the under line of the outside falling mould; the top lines are only drawn parallel to the under side to the thickness of the rail.

In applying them to practice, draw a line *t p* to touch the mould in two places; this will represent the edge of the Plank, next square over several lines, as *p q* where the moulds intersect, and at *t s r,* square over on the plank lines corresponding with these, and mark off from the edge of the plank the distances *p q* and *t s* on one side, and *t r* on the other, make the moulds agree with these points, each one on its proper side, and mark off the rail; the plank being of a sufficient thickness to allow for the saw curfs will when cut out, and twisted, become square, and of the proper size.

PLATE 36

Drawing Plans and Elevations.

In this Plate is given a Plan and Elevation of a small house; the Student in drawing a Plan, will suppose the building to be raised just above the principal floor, and the wall made level all round; and draw his plan to resemble it as near as possible; placing the partitions, doors, and windows in their proper places; the stairs should be drawn for the whole story to show where the landing for the next story will be; in drawing the ground plan it will considerably enliven the drawing to give the appearance of a shadow on one side of the wall, by drawing one line thicker than the other; to do this he will suppose the light to come from the left hand upper corner of the drawing, and make the lines on the right hand and lower side of the walls and partitions thick, and the other sides thin lines: this will be better understood by closely inspecting the plans that follow.

PLATE 36

PLATE 37

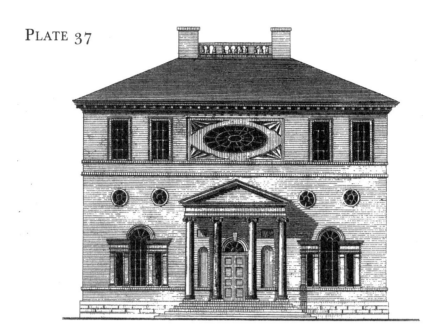

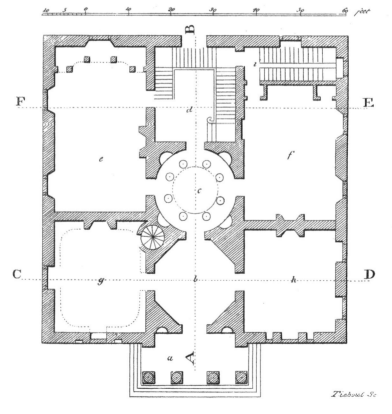

PLATE 37

Is a Design for a large building; the dotted lines A B, C D and E F show the place on the ground plan, through which the sections in the three following plates are drawn the letters on the sections corresponding with the letters on the plans.

The Plan in this Plate is for the principal story or first floor, and may be disposed of as follows, viz.

a Portico.

b Hall. This is an octagon with the ceiling vaulted, and includes in its height the mezanine, or small story between the two principal ones. *See section of Plate* 38.

c Vestibule. This is lighted from a sky-light, and at the second story has a gallery which gives a communication with the different rooms. *See section of Plate* 38.

d Stairs.

e Salloon. This room includes in its height the mezanine, and has a music gallery. *See section of Plate* 40.

f Dining room, with a recess for a side-board.

g Library.

h Breakfast parlour.

i Back stairs.

Plate 38

Contains a section of the same building as the foregoing, with the plan for the Cellar or basement story.

In drawing a section, the Student will pay strict attention that it agrees in all its parts with the plans for the different stories, and that the section represents the building as it were cut through from top to bottom, on the line of the plan, from which it is taken; a little liberty indeed may be taken with stairs, as when the section cuts through them, to represent half of them would not be as clear as if all was shown.

The plan in this Plate may be disposed of as follows, viz.

a Maid servants' room. The small stairs gives a communication with the mezanine, and chamber over the library.

b Housekeeper's room.

c Servants' hall.

d Back stairs.

e Kitchen.

f Men servants' room.

g b and *i* Beer and Wine cellars, &c.

PLATE 38

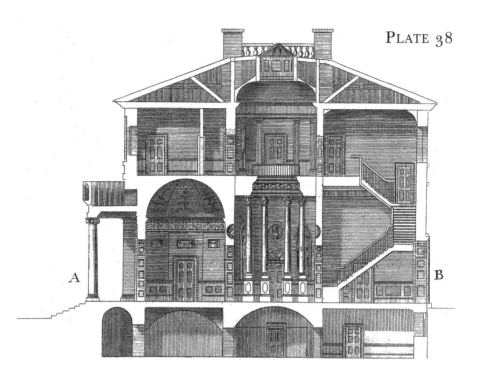

A   B

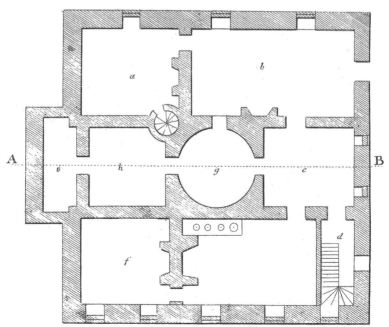

A   B

PLATE 39

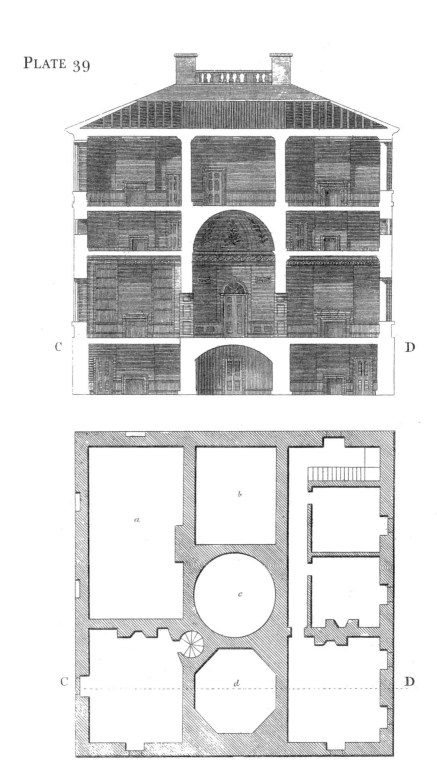

C   D

PLATE 39

The same building continued. The plan is for the Mezanine or small story between the two principal stories; of this *a b c* and *d* are the upper parts of the Saloon, Stairs, Vestibule and Hall; the others are small rooms for servants, &c.

Mezanine stories, or as they are sometimes called mezetti, are of use in a large building, where some of the rooms are so large as to require more height than common rooms, to be well proportioned; the mezanine being thrown into the height of the large rooms. And they also afford convenient chambers for servants, more particularly those whose business it is to attend on the master and mistress, by affording a room immediately under the chambers occupied by them, with a private stairs for communication: were it not for this, in very large buildings, the servants would frequently be unavoidably lodged at a considerable distance from the heads of the family.

PLATE 40

The same continued. The plan is for the second story, in which

a is the Vestibule, with a gallery of communication from the stairs to the different rooms.

b and *c* two Chambers, with each an antichamber or dressing room; the rest are private chambers, except *d* and *e* which are stairs.

In these plans it has been more my object to throw as great a variety into a small compass as was readily practicable, than to give eligible plans for the builder, thereby aiming at instruction for the Student, which indeed has been my object throughout this work.

PLATE 40

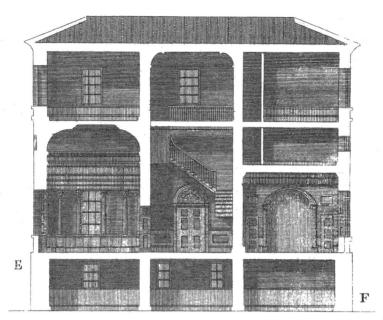

E   F

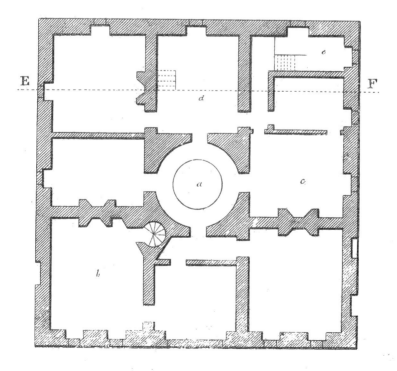

E   F

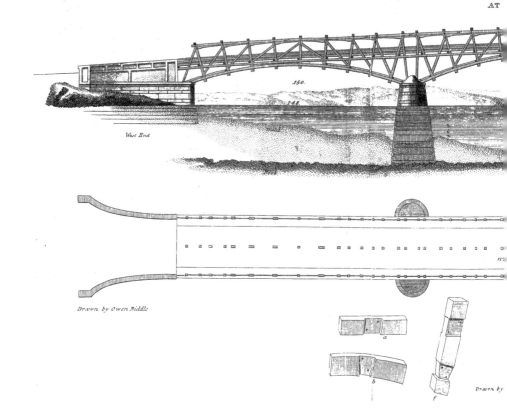

West End

150.

148.

Drawn by Owen Riddle

a

b

f

Drawn by

PLATE 41

RIVER SCHUYLKILL

PHIA

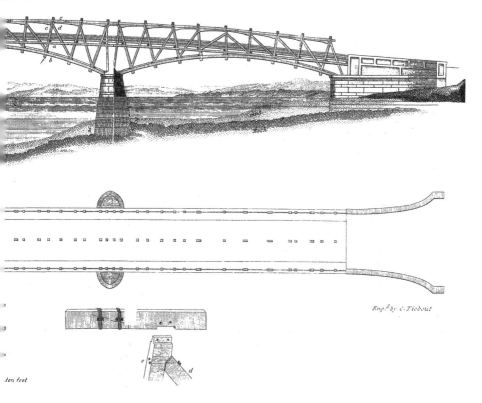

Engd by C.Tiebout

ten feet

The following Plates I have been induced to give, as containing four different varieties in Architecture; of these it is difficult to say which is the most perfect.

Plate 41.

Contains a draft of the Frame of the Bridge lately erected, by a Company incorporated for that purpose, over the Schuylkill, at the West End of High or Market Street; with a section of the Bed of that River.

The westernmost pier of this Bridge is sunk in a depth of water, unexampled in Hydraulic-Architecture, in any part of the world; the top of the rock on which it stands being 41 feet 9 inches below common high tides. Both piers were built within Coffer-dams. The dam for the Western pier was of original and peculiar construction; the design furnished by William Weston Esq. of Gainsborough in England, a celebrated Hydraulic engineer. An idea of its magnitude may be formed when it is known that 800,000 feet of timber, (board measure) were unavoidably employed *in* and *about* it. It was executed, under the orders of the Building Committee of the Board, consisting of the President and four, and sometimes 5 Directors (to whom the master workmen express great obligations) by Samuel Robinson of this city. Every disadvantage to which such difficult undertakings are subject (the rock being, in sundry parts, nearly bare, and affording no footing for the piles) opposed the progress of this. So that it could not be ready for the commencement of the masonry, until the 25th of December, when the first stone was laid; and the work continued in a severe Winter, to the height then proposed.

The stone work was done by Thomas Vickers, under the orders, and with the advice and constant attention of the same Committee; assisted, on emergencies, by all the members of the Board, and the Treasurer, who was eminently useful on every occasion. The *masonry* is executed on a plan suggested to the mason, uncommon, if not new. The walls of the Abutments and

Wings are *perpendicular,* without *buttresses*; and supported by interior *offsets.* These are found completely competent to support the pressure of the filling, without *battering* or *contreforts.* The *Abutments* are 18 feet thick. The *Wing walls* 9 feet at the foundations; retiring by offsets, 'till at the parapets they are only 18 inches. The Eastern abutment and wing walls are founded on a rock. Those on the Western side, are built on piles. There are upwards of 7,500 tons of masonry in the Western pier. Many of the stones, composing both piers, weigh from 3 to 12 tons. A number of massive chains are stretched, in various positions, across the piers. These are worked in with the masonry; the exterior whereof is clamped, and finished in the most substantial and workmanlike manner.

The *Frame* of the superstructure was designed and erected by Timothy Palmer of Newbury-port in Massachusetts. It is a masterly piece of workmanship; combining in its principles, that of King posts and Braces, with that of a Stone arch. Half of each post, with the brace between them, will form the vousseur of an arch; and lines through the middle of each post, would describe the radii, or joints. The letters *a b c* &c. in the draught, refer to the same letters below; where the manner of connecting the timbers together, is shown on a larger scale. The position of the letters are the same, with respect to each piece, in both places. Two of these, *a* and *b,* are double, or in two thicknesses. There are 3 sections of the Frame, similar to the one represented. That in the middle divides the space into two equal parts. So that those passing, in opposite directions, are prevented from interfering with each other. The Platform for travelling rises only 8 feet from a horizontal line; and the Top, or Cap pieces, are parallel to this. Of the sections the middle one has the most pressure; owing to the weight of transportation being thrown nearer to that section than towards the sides; to which the foot-ways prevent its approach. These foot-ways are 5 feet in width; elevated above the carriage-ways, and neatly protected by posts and chains. T. Palmer is the original inventor of *this kind* of Wooden bridge-Architecture. He permitted with much candour, considerable alterations in the plan, on which he had erected several bridges in New-England. These were accommodatory to the intended Cover, and were so much approved by him, that he considers the Schuylkill Bridge superstructure the most perfect of any he has built.

After the erection of the Frame, the Editor was employed by the President and Directors to perform the workmanship of the covering, agreeably to a design furnished by them to him: this design of the Cover being original, it is more surprising that it has not many faults, than that few, if any, can be found. Especially as an accommodation to the Frame, created unavoidable difficulties. The Editor was permitted to make some additions, with the approbation of the Building Committee. He feels himself grateful for the assistance he has had; and in participating with those who preceded him, in the approbation of the work, by the Board and their Committee. At their suggestion, the under work of the side covering is done imitation of mason-ry, by sprinkling the work with stone dust on the painting while fresh. The smalting or sprinkling was performed with so much ease and cheapness, that it is hoped it will introduce a like mode of ornamenting and protecting the surface of wooden elevations, of other descriptions, where protection and ornament are required.

Commodious Wharves, on each side of the river, have been made by the Company; not only to protect the foundations of the abutments and wings, but with a view to profit. They co-operate with the other improvements, to give a new and interesting front to our city.

It is a peculiar and interesting fact, that (except the valuable assistance ren-dered in its commencement by W. Weston, who was then about returning to England) no scientific engineer has been employed, in any part of this great undertaking. Neither the Board, or their Committee who have been con-stantly and actively engaged in all stages of the work, profess a scientific knowledge of Hydraulic Architecture; though they have now gained much practical experience. Yet difficulties have been encountered and overcome, which would have called forth the talents, and practical knowledge, of the ablest engineer. The mechanics and workmen (T. Palmer and his assistants excepted) had, from the beginning of the undertaking, new and unknown branches of their business to learn. Even T. Palmer is *self taught* in the art of wooden-bridge building; though he has carried it to such high perfection. It is however believed that this bridge, in all its parts, both of masonry and wood work, will not suffer by a comparison with one so composed, in any part of the world. Its workmanship and materials will stand the test of the most rigid scrutiny. Both the plan and its execution, reflect credit upon those concerned in the enterprise. So far as I have information, this is now the only *covered* wooden Bridge, in any Country, except, perhaps, one over the Limmat, built by the same Swiss carpenter who erected that of Schauffhausen, since destroyed. I have frequently seen and carefully inspected the draughts of this much celebrated Bridge, and I am confident that any intelligent and candid Architect, on examining the principles of both, would give a decided preference to the Schuylkill Bridge. The design is more simple, its strength is greater, its parts are better combined and more assistant to each other, and there is no useless timber, or unnecessary complexity in any part.

What I have just observed, as to those engaged in the direction or execution of the work of the Schuylkill Bridge, is not intended as adulatory, or disparaging to any persons. But I have an ardent hope that others, in similar undertakings, will be animated by their successful example; when labouring under the same, or greater disadvantages, arising from the want of experience and scientific professors of Architecture; although where these can be had, for great undertakings, they ought, undoubtedly, to be employed.

As a well-wisher to all public improvements, as a mechanic and one employed to close this eminently useful erection, I think it my duty to mention, and feel a sensible satisfaction in adding to the foregoing account—

That I have experienced the important advantages of ready and beneficial advice, clear, prompt and explicit orders, and timely and ample supplies. Not a moment has been lost by delay and hesitation in directions, want of provision of materials, or deficiency in punctuality of payment. This has been constantly the case, through the whole progress of the business, as the workmen preceding me in its more difficult stages, have testified. Though heavy expenditures have been inevitably required, the greatest attention to economy has been practised.

No interested or personal motives induce me to mention these circumstances. They are exemplary; and essential to ensure the completion of any extensive enterprise. To them, I am persuaded is to be chiefly attributed, the success of this arduous work. From inattention, or incapacity in these indispensable requisites, many public, as well as private undertakings in all countries have failed; and communities, and the individuals employed in them, have been involved in disappointment and distress; if not in irretrievable ruin.

The Bridge has been 6 years in building, and cost about 275,000 dolls. including the cash moiety of the purchase of the site; for which 40,000 dolls. were paid to the City Corporation, half in cash and half in Bridge shares.

	ft.	in.
Length of the Bridge	550	00
Abutments and wing walls	750	00
Total length	1300	00
Span of small arches each	150	00
Ditto of middle arch	194	10
Width of the bridge	42	00
Curvature of the middle arch	12	00
Ditto of small arches	10	00
Curvature or rise of the carriage way or road	8	00
Height in the clear over carriage way	13	00
Ditto from the surface of the river to the carriage way	31	00
Thickness of the pier	20	00
Length of ditto	62	00
Depth of water to the rock at the western pier	41	9
Ditto at the eastern pier	21	00

Amount of toll when the work began for
the year 1799, arising from
the floating bridge   5,000 Dolls.

Present amount of toll on an average (1805)
the rates of toll in several instances being
lower than over the old floating bridge   13,600

PLATE 42

The Bank of Pennsylvania.

This beautiful building is entirely of Marble and is a neat specimen of the
Ionic Order, taken from an ancient Greek Temple; the design was given by,
and the building erected under the superintendence of Benjamin H. Latrobe.
The front extends 51 ft in width, and the whole building, including the
Porticos front and back, is 125 ft in depth. This building was three years in
hand, and was finished in the year 1799.

PLATE 42

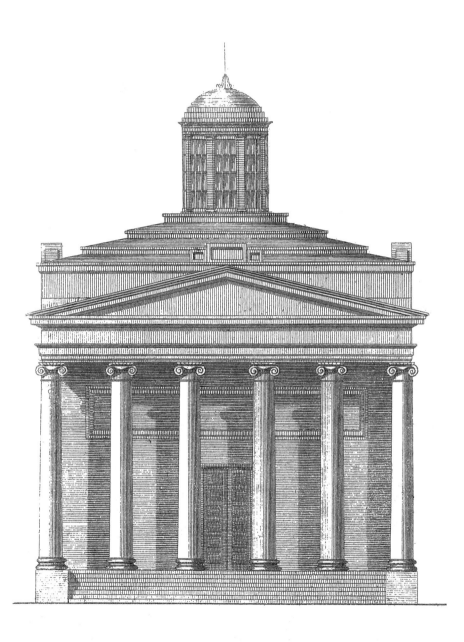

PLATE 43

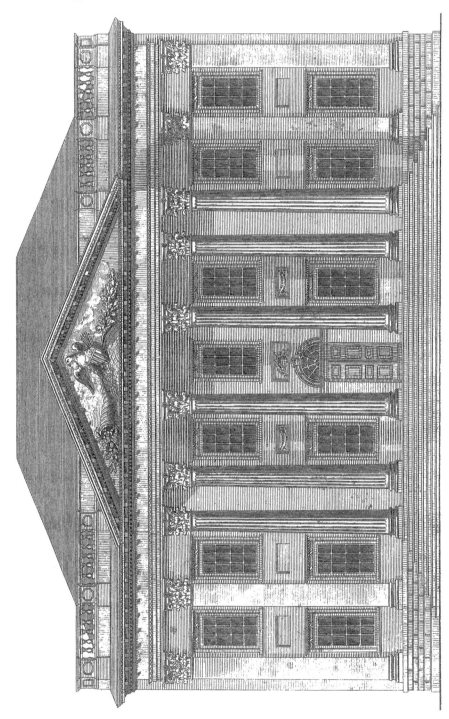

PLATE 43

Bank of the United States.

This superb Building is an elegant specimen of the Corinthian Order; the proportions taken from a Roman Temple called the Maison Quarree, at Nismes, in the south of France. The front extends 94 ft by 72 deep exclusive of the Portico. The design was given by Samuel Blodget of this city, and was built about the year 1795.

PLATE 44

Contains an elevation of the Steeple of Christ Church in Second Street, which for the justness of its proportions, simplicity and symmetry of its parts is allowed by good judges to be equal if not superior in beauty to any Steeple of the spire kind, either in Europe or America. It was erected in the year 1755 by Robert Smith, who some time after took out the sills of the wooden part which had begun to decay, and replaced them by others.

The superstructure of this steeple is composed of three distinct well-proportioned parts of Architecture, the first story, with its small Pediments and Attics, forming one; the octagonal part, with its ogee formed dome, being the second; and the spire and its pedestal, the third. These three parts are very dissimilar, no one having any thing in it that is common to the others; and yet they agree very well with each other, forming one complete and consistent whole.

PLATE 44

Whole height 190 feet

C. Tiebout Sc.

A DICTIONARY OF TERMS
USED IN ARCHITECTURE.

A.

ABACUS, the upper member of a column, which serves as a covering to the capital; to the Tuscan, Doric and Ionic, it is square; to the modern Ionic and Corinthian, each side is arched, or cut inwards, and is decorated in the centre with a flower or other ornament.

ACANTHUS, a plant, whose leaves form an ornament in the Corinthian capital, and are said to have originally given rise to that order.

ACROTERIA, a kind of base, placed on the angles of pediments, usually for the support of statues, &c.

ALÆ, Ailes, also passages in theatres, houses, &c. the space between the walls and the columns.

AMPHITHEATRE, a place for exhibiting shows, very spacious, of a round or oval figure, with many seats rising on every side. The area in the middle was called *Arena,* because it was covered with sand, or sawdust, to prevent slipping, and to absorb blood.

ANNULET, a small square moulding, which serves to crown or accompany a larger, and to separate the flutings in columns.

ANTÆ, a species of pilasters on the extremity of a wall, usually having no diminution, nor do the mouldings of their capitals or bases always resemble those of the columns.

AQUÆDUCT, an artificial canal, built for the conveyance of water from one place to another, either running under ground, or rising above it.

ARCH, part of a circle or ellipsis.

ARCHITRAVE, the lowest principal member of an entablature, lying immediately upon the abacus of the capital.

ASTRAGAL, a small round moulding with two annulets.

ATTIC BASE, Ionic Base.

B.

BALUSTER, small columns, or pillars of wood, stone, &c. used on terraces or tops of buildings for ornament, and to support railing, and, when continued, form a *balustrade.*

BANISTER, the supports of an hand-rail of stairs.

BAND, a general term for a low, flat, or square member.

BASE, the lower and projecting part of a column and pedestal.

BUTMENT, or *Abutment,* supporters, or props, on or against which the feet of arches rest.

BUTTRESS, a kind of butment, built sometimes archwise, as to Gothic buildings; a mass of stone or brick work, serving to prop or support buildings, walls, &c. on the outside, where their great height or weight require additional strength.

C.

CAPITAL, the uppermost member of a column, which is a crown or head thereto, placed immediately over the *shaft*, and under the *architrave*; no column is complete without a capital, which has a distinguishing character for each order.—Tuscan and Doric capitals consist of mouldings; Ionic and Corinthian capitals, of leaves and other ornaments.

CARTOUCHE, an ornament in sculpture representing a scroll of paper, &c.

CARYATIDES, a kind of order in Architecture, in which a female figure is applied instead of a pillar; the origin of which is thus handed down by Vitruvius: the inhabitants of Caria, a city of Peloponnesus, made a league with the Persians against their own nation; but the Persians being worsted, they were afterwards besieged by the victorious party, their city taken and reduced to ashes, the men put to the sword, and the women carried away captives. To perpetuate the memory of this victory, the conquerors caused public edifices to be erected, in which, as a mark of degradation and servility, the figures of the captives were used instead of columns, thus handing down to posterity their servility and punishment. When figures of the male sex are used, they are called *Persians* or *Perses*.

CAVETTO, a concave moulding of one quarter of a circle.

CAULICOLI, the little twists or volutes under the flower on the abacus in the Corinthian capital, represent the twisted tops of the acanthus stalks; are called also *Helices*.

CELL, in an ancient temple, is the inclosed space within the walls.

CENTER or *Centre,* the support of an arch while the masons are building it.

CINCTURE, a ring, list, or fillet, at the top and bottom of the shaft of the column.

CIRCUS, a large building for exhibiting equestrian exercises in.

COFFER-DAM, a large frame constructed for the purpose of erecting works on the bottom of deep waters; the Coffer-dam being water tight and surrounding the place intended to work on, is emptied of the water and leaves the bottom bare.

COLLAR-BEAM, timbers placed across a roof from the middle of one rafter to another.

COLLARIN, or *Collarino,* the neck or frize of a Tuscan or Doric capital.

COLONNADE, a series or continuation of columns.

COLUMN, a round pillar used in Architecture, to adorn or support. Columns are of four kinds; the *Tuscan, Doric, Ionic,* and *Corinthian,* each of which has its particular proportion. The term includes the base and the capital.

CONGE, a small moulding, which serves to separate larger ones, called also *List* or *Annulet.*

CONSOLE, an ornament cut on the key-stone of arches, with a projection, capable of supporting busts, vases, &c.

CONTOUR, the outline of a figure, or piece of Architecture.

COPING *of a wall,* the top or covering made sloping to throw off water.

CORBEILLE, carved work, representing a basket with fruits or flowers, serving as a finish to some other ornament. It sometimes is applied to the vase of the Corinthian capital, the word originally meaning a basket.

CORINTHIAN *order,* one of the four orders of Architecture.

CORNICE, the upper assemblage of members in an entablature, commencing at the frize; each order has its particular cornice, with suitable enrichments. To the

Tuscan it is quite plain; to the *Doric* are added *guttæ,* or bells in the *soffit:* the *Ionic* has plain modillions; the *Corinthian* is much enriched, and has modillions.

CORONA, a large flat and strong member in a cornice, called also the *Drift,* or *Larmier,* its use is to screen the under parts of the work, and, from its shape, to prevent the water running down the column; it has always a large projection to answer its proposed use.

CORRIDOR, a gallery or passage in large buildings, which leads to distant apartments.

CUPOLA, a round roof or dome, in the form of an inverted cup.

CYMA, *Cima,* or *Cymatium,* a species of moulding, which is generally the upper one to an entablature. There are two sorts of this moulding, the *cyma recta* and *cyma reversa,* which is commonly called an *ogee.*

D.

DENTELE, an ornament resembling teeth, used in Ionic and Corinthian cornices.

DIE, the square or naked piece in a pedestal, that part which is between the base and the capital.

DOME, a spherical roof.—See *Cupola.*

DORIC *order,* one of the four orders of Architecture.

DROPS or *Guttæ,* in the Doric entablature, are small inverted pyramids or cones, immediately under the triglyph.

E.

ECHINUS, is properly the egg and anchor ornament peculiar to the *Ionic* capital; it is sometimes used for the whole member instead of *ovalo.*

ENTABLATURE, an ornament or assemblage of parts, supported by a column or pilaster

over the capital: each order of columns has a peculiar entablature divided into three principal parts; the *architrave,* which is divided into two or more *facia,* and rests upon the capital. The *frize* is next, and may be plain or ornamented. The *cornice* is the top or crowning part.

F.

FAÇADE, the front view or elevation of a building.

FACIA, a flat member in the entablature of an order, representing a band or broad fillet in an architrave; if divided, these divisions are called the first facia, the second facia, &c.

FILLET. See *Annulet.*

FLUTINGS, the hollows or channels, which are cut perpendicularly in columns by way of ornament, and which should always both begin and end in the shaft, near the extremity of the apophyges; though there are examples to the contrary. When flutings are used the capital should be enriched.

FOLIAGE, an assemblage of leaves.

FRETT, an ornament laid on plain narrow surfaces formed by one or more fillets running along in a zig-zag direction, generally in right angles, and keeping a space between each fillet equal in width to the fillet itself.

FRIZE, or *Frise,* the middle member of an entablature, having the architrave below, and the cornice above.

FRONTISPIECE, sometimes signifies the whole face or aspect of a building, but is more properly applied to the decorated entrance of a house.

FUST, the shaft of a column, or that part which is between the base and the capital.

G.

GIRDERS, large pieces of timber in flooring, laid from one wall to another, when the distance is too great for common joists.

GLYPHS, the perpendicular channels cut in the *triglyphs* of the Doric frize.

GOTHIC, a peculiar style of Architecture, distinct from the Grecian or Roman, derived from the Goths, or rather from the Saracens.

GUILOCHES, ornaments made by circular fillets crossing and recrossing each other, generally encompassing a patera or flower.

H.

HAMMER-BEAM, when the ceiling of a large building is vaulted, the tie-beam of the roof is broken in the middle and raised to admit of the curvature of the ceiling, the middle of the beam being secured to the collar-beam it is then called a hammer-beam.

I.

IMPOST, a facia or small cornice which crowns a pier or pilaster, and from which an arch springs.

INSULATED, standing alone, or detached from any contiguous building, &c.

INTERCOLUMNIATION, the space between two columns.

IONIC *order,* one of the four orders of Architecture.

K.

KEY-STONE, the highest stone of an arch, to which a projection is usually given, and which is sometimes cut in ornaments.

KING-POST, the middle upright post in a set of principal rafters in large roofs; being supported by the rafters it supports the middle of the beam, and keeps it from sagging.

L.

LACUNARIÆ, pannels or coffers in ceilings, or in the soffits of cornices, &c.

M.

METOPE, the interval or square space between the triglyphs in the Doric frize.

MEZZANINE, or *Mezzetti,* small or low stories between principal ones, used as servants' apartments.

MINUTE, an *architectonic measure,* the lower diameter of a column divided into sixty parts, each part is a *minute.*

MODILLION, an ornament resembling a bracket, in the Ionic and Corinthian cornices.

MOULDINGS, those parts which project beyond the base or perpendicular face of a wall, column, &c. intended only for ornament, whether round, flat, or curved: the regular mouldings are, 1st, the *list,* or *annulet*; 2d, the *astragal,* or *bead*; 3d, the *cyma reversa,* or ogee; 4th, the *cyma recta*; 5th, the *cavetto,* or hollow; 6th, the *ovolo,* or quarter round; 7th, the *scotia*; 8th, the *torus.*

MUTULE, an ornament in the Doric cornice, answering to a *modillion* in the Ionic and Corinthian entablatures.

N.

NICHE, a cavity or hollow in a wall for statues, &c.

O.

OBELISK, a tall pyramid.

OGEE, a *cyma reversa.*

ORDER, in Architecture, a column entire, consisting of *base, shaft,* and *capital,* with an *entablature.*

OVA, or *ovum.* See *Echinus.*

OVOLO, a moulding which projects one quarter of a circle, called also a *quarter round.*

P.

PEDESTAL, a square body on which columns, &c. are placed.

PEDIMENT, a low triangular ornament in the front of buildings, and over doors, windows, &c.

PIER, a kind of pilaster or buttress, to support, strengthen, or ornament; the pier of a bridge, is the foot or support of the arch. The wall between windows or doors. Also square pillars of stone or brick, to which gates are hung.

PERISTYLE, a range of columns or colonnade, within a court or building like a cloister.

PIAZZA, a continued arched way or vaulting, under which to walk, &c.

PILASTER, a square pillar or column, usually placed against a wall.

PILLAR, this word is generally used in Architecture, in common with *column,* though, strictly speaking, they are different; thus the supporters in Gothic Architecture are pillars, but can never be properly termed columns, varying in shape and every particular from the latter.

PLANCERE, a reversed plan of a cornice or other moulding; or a view of the same from below.

PLAT-BAND, any flat square moulding with little projection; the different facias of an architrave are called plat-bands; the

same is applied to the list between flutings, &c.

PLINTH, the lower member of a base.

PORTICO, a continued range of columns covered at top, to shelter from the weather; also, a common name to buildings which have covered walks supported by pillars.

PRINCE-POST, a post placed upright in framing of principal rafters between the king-post and the end of the tie-beam, giving additional support to the tie-beam.

PRINCIPAL RAFTERS, large roofs are supported by sets of framing placed at from 8 to 10 feet apart, these frames are generally composed of tie-beams, king-posts, prince-posts, braces or trusses, and rafters.

PROFILE, the outline or contour of any building, &c.

PURLINS, square pieces of timber laid from one set of principal rafters to another; on these are laid the jack-rafters or small rafters to receive the covering.

PYRAMID, a structure, which, from a square, triangular, or other base, rises gradually to a point.

Q.

QUARTER ROUND, a moulding. See *Ovolo.*

QUOINS, stones or other materials put in the angles of buildings to strengthen them.

R.

RELIEVO, signifies the projection of any carved ornament.

ROTUNDA, a building which is round both within and without.

RUSTIC, the term is applied to those stones in a building which are hatched or picked in holes, resembling a natural rough appearance.

S.

SALOON, a lofty, vaulted, spacious hall or apartment.

SCOTIA, a hollow moulding used in bases to columns.

SECTION OF A BUILDING, represents it as if cut perpendicularly from the roof downwards, and serves to show the internal decorations and distribution.

SHAFT, the trunk or body of a column between the base and the capital.

SOFFIT, the under part or ceiling of a cornice, which is usually ornamented; the under part of the *corona* is called the *Soffit*; the word is also applied to the ceiling of an arch, the under side of an architrave, &c.

T.

TENIA, the upper member of the Doric architrave; a kind of *listel*.

TIE-BEAMS, large timbers forming the base line of a set of principal rafters.

TORUS, or *Tore,* a large semicircular moulding, used in the base of columns.

TRANSOM, a piece placed over a door when there is to be an opening for light immediately over the door; when the opening over is circular it is generally called an impost.

TRIGLYPH, an ornament peculiar to the Doric frize.

TRUSS or *Brace,* pieces of timber used in framing to support the middle of any great span.

TUSCAN *Order,* one of the four orders of Architecture.

TYMPAN, the flat surface or space within a pediment.

V.

VASE, the body of a Corinthian capital, also an ornament used in Architecture, &c.

VAULT, an arched roof, the stones or materials of which are so placed as to support each other.

VOLUTE, the scroll or spiral horn, used in Ionic capitals.

W.

WALL-PLATE, a piece of timber laid on the top of a wall on which is laid the joist and framing of the roof.

Z.

ZOGLE, or *Soccolo,* a low square member, which serves to elevate a statue, vase, &c. also when a range of columns is erected on one continued high *plinth,* it is called a *Zocle*; it differs from a pedestal, being without base or cornice.

A CATALOG OF SELECTED
DOVER BOOKS
IN ALL FIELDS OF INTEREST

A CATALOG OF SELECTED DOVER
BOOKS IN ALL FIELDS OF INTEREST

100 BEST-LOVED POEMS, Edited by Philip Smith. "The Passionate Shepherd to His Love," "Shall I compare thee to a summer's day?" "Death, be not proud," "The Raven," "The Road Not Taken," plus works by Blake, Wordsworth, Byron, Shelley, Keats, many others. 96pp. 5³⁄₁₆ x 8¼. 0-486-28553-7

100 SMALL HOUSES OF THE THIRTIES, Brown-Blodgett Company. Exterior photographs and floor plans for 100 charming structures. Illustrations of models accompanied by descriptions of interiors, color schemes, closet space, and other amenities. 200 illustrations. 112pp. 8⅜ x 11. 0-486-44131-8

1000 TURN-OF-THE-CENTURY HOUSES: With Illustrations and Floor Plans, Herbert C. Chivers. Reproduced from a rare edition, this showcase of homes ranges from cottages and bungalows to sprawling mansions. Each house is meticulously illustrated and accompanied by complete floor plans. 256pp. 9⅜ x 12¼.
0-486-45596-3

101 GREAT AMERICAN POEMS, Edited by The American Poetry & Literacy Project. Rich treasury of verse from the 19th and 20th centuries includes works by Edgar Allan Poe, Robert Frost, Walt Whitman, Langston Hughes, Emily Dickinson, T. S. Eliot, other notables. 96pp. 5³⁄₁₆ x 8¼. 0-486-40158-8

101 GREAT SAMURAI PRINTS, Utagawa Kuniyoshi. Kuniyoshi was a master of the warrior woodblock print — and these 18th-century illustrations represent the pinnacle of his craft. Full-color portraits of renowned Japanese samurais pulse with movement, passion, and remarkably fine detail. 112pp. 8⅜ x 11. 0-486-46523-3

ABC OF BALLET, Janet Grosser. Clearly worded, abundantly illustrated little guide defines basic ballet-related terms: arabesque, battement, pas de chat, relevé, sissonne, many others. Pronunciation guide included. Excellent primer. 48pp. 4³⁄₁₆ x 5¾.
0-486-40871-X

ACCESSORIES OF DRESS: An Illustrated Encyclopedia, Katherine Lester and Bess Viola Oerke. Illustrations of hats, veils, wigs, cravats, shawls, shoes, gloves, and other accessories enhance an engaging commentary that reveals the humor and charm of the many-sided story of accessorized apparel. 644 figures and 59 plates. 608pp. 6⅛ x 9¼.
0-486-43378-1

ADVENTURES OF HUCKLEBERRY FINN, Mark Twain. Join Huck and Jim as their boyhood adventures along the Mississippi River lead them into a world of excitement, danger, and self-discovery. Humorous narrative, lyrical descriptions of the Mississippi valley, and memorable characters. 224pp. 5³⁄₁₆ x 8¼. 0-486-28061-6

ALICE STARMORE'S BOOK OF FAIR ISLE KNITTING, Alice Starmore. A noted designer from the region of Scotland's Fair Isle explores the history and techniques of this distinctive, stranded-color knitting style and provides copious illustrated instructions for 14 original knitwear designs. 208pp. 8⅜ x 10⅞. 0-486-47218-3

ALICE'S ADVENTURES IN WONDERLAND, Lewis Carroll. Beloved classic about a little girl lost in a topsy-turvy land and her encounters with the White Rabbit, March Hare, Mad Hatter, Cheshire Cat, and other delightfully improbable characters. 42 illustrations by Sir John Tenniel. 96pp. 5³⁄₁₆ x 8¼. 0-486-27543-4

AMERICA'S LIGHTHOUSES: An Illustrated History, Francis Ross Holland. Profusely illustrated fact-filled survey of American lighthouses since 1716. Over 200 stations — East, Gulf, and West coasts, Great Lakes, Hawaii, Alaska, Puerto Rico, the Virgin Islands, and the Mississippi and St. Lawrence Rivers. 240pp. 8 x 10¾.
0-486-25576-X

AN ENCYCLOPEDIA OF THE VIOLIN, Alberto Bachmann. Translated by Frederick H. Martens. Introduction by Eugene Ysaye. First published in 1925, this renowned reference remains unsurpassed as a source of essential information, from construction and evolution to repertoire and technique. Includes a glossary and 73 illustrations. 496pp. 6½ x 9¼. 0-486-46618-3

ANIMALS: 1,419 Copyright-Free Illustrations of Mammals, Birds, Fish, Insects, etc., Selected by Jim Harter. Selected for its visual impact and ease of use, this outstanding collection of wood engravings presents over 1,000 species of animals in extremely lifelike poses. Includes mammals, birds, reptiles, amphibians, fish, insects, and other invertebrates. 284pp. 9 x 12. 0-486-23766-4

THE ANNALS, Tacitus. Translated by Alfred John Church and William Jackson Brodribb. This vital chronicle of Imperial Rome, written by the era's great historian, spans A.D. 14-68 and paints incisive psychological portraits of major figures, from Tiberius to Nero. 416pp. 5³⁄₁₆ x 8¼. 0-486-45236-0

ANTIGONE, Sophocles. Filled with passionate speeches and sensitive probing of moral and philosophical issues, this powerful and often-performed Greek drama reveals the grim fate that befalls the children of Oedipus. Footnotes. 64pp. 5³⁄₁₆ x 8 ¼. 0-486-27804-2

ART DECO DECORATIVE PATTERNS IN FULL COLOR, Christian Stoll. Reprinted from a rare 1910 portfolio, 160 sensuous and exotic images depict a breathtaking array of florals, geometrics, and abstracts — all elegant in their stark simplicity. 64pp. 8⅜ x 11. 0-486-44862-2

THE ARTHUR RACKHAM TREASURY: 86 Full-Color Illustrations, Arthur Rackham. Selected and Edited by Jeff A. Menges. A stunning treasury of 86 full-page plates span the famed English artist's career, from *Rip Van Winkle* (1905) to masterworks such as *Undine, A Midsummer Night's Dream,* and *Wind in the Willows* (1939). 96pp. 8⅜ x 11.
0-486-44685-9

THE AUTHENTIC GILBERT & SULLIVAN SONGBOOK, W. S. Gilbert and A. S. Sullivan. The most comprehensive collection available, this songbook includes selections from every one of Gilbert and Sullivan's light operas. Ninety-two numbers are presented uncut and unedited, and in their original keys. 410pp. 9 x 12.
0-486-23482-7

THE AWAKENING, Kate Chopin. First published in 1899, this controversial novel of a New Orleans wife's search for love outside a stifling marriage shocked readers. Today, it remains a first-rate narrative with superb characterization. New introductory Note. 128pp. 5³⁄₁₆ x 8¼. 0-486-27786-0

BASIC DRAWING, Louis Priscilla. Beginning with perspective, this commonsense manual progresses to the figure in movement, light and shade, anatomy, drapery, composition, trees and landscape, and outdoor sketching. Black-and-white illustrations throughout. 128pp. 8⅜ x 11. 0-486-45815-6

Browse over 9,000 books at www.doverpublications.com

CATALOG OF DOVER BOOKS

THE BATTLES THAT CHANGED HISTORY, Fletcher Pratt. Historian profiles 16 crucial conflicts, ancient to modern, that changed the course of Western civilization. Gripping accounts of battles led by Alexander the Great, Joan of Arc, Ulysses S. Grant, other commanders. 27 maps. 352pp. 5⅜ x 8½. 0-486-41129-X

BEETHOVEN'S LETTERS, Ludwig van Beethoven. Edited by Dr. A. C. Kalischer. Features 457 letters to fellow musicians, friends, greats, patrons, and literary men. Reveals musical thoughts, quirks of personality, insights, and daily events. Includes 15 plates. 410pp. 5⅜ x 8½. 0-486-22769-3

BERNICE BOBS HER HAIR AND OTHER STORIES, F. Scott Fitzgerald. This brilliant anthology includes 6 of Fitzgerald's most popular stories: "The Diamond as Big as the Ritz," the title tale, "The Offshore Pirate," "The Ice Palace," "The Jelly Bean," and "May Day." 176pp. 5⅜ x 8½. 0-486-47049-0

BESLER'S BOOK OF FLOWERS AND PLANTS: 73 Full-Color Plates from Hortus Eystettensis, 1613, Basilius Besler. Here is a selection of magnificent plates from the *Hortus Eystettensis,* which vividly illustrated and identified the plants, flowers, and trees that thrived in the legendary German garden at Eichstätt. 80pp. 8⅜ x 11. 0-486-46005-3

THE BOOK OF KELLS, Edited by Blanche Cirker. Painstakingly reproduced from a rare facsimile edition, this volume contains full-page decorations, portraits, illustrations, plus a sampling of textual leaves with exquisite calligraphy and ornamentation. 32 full-color illustrations. 32pp. 9⅜ x 12¼. 0-486-24345-1

THE BOOK OF THE CROSSBOW: With an Additional Section on Catapults and Other Siege Engines, Ralph Payne-Gallwey. Fascinating study traces history and use of crossbow as military and sporting weapon, from Middle Ages to modern times. Also covers related weapons: balistas, catapults, Turkish bows, more. Over 240 illustrations. 400pp. 7¼ x 10⅛. 0-486-28720-3

THE BUNGALOW BOOK: Floor Plans and Photos of 112 Houses, 1910, Henry L. Wilson. Here are 112 of the most popular and economic blueprints of the early 20th century — plus an illustration or photograph of each completed house. A wonderful time capsule that still offers a wealth of valuable insights. 160pp. 8⅜ x 11. 0-486-45104-6

THE CALL OF THE WILD, Jack London. A classic novel of adventure, drawn from London's own experiences as a Klondike adventurer, relating the story of a heroic dog caught in the brutal life of the Alaska Gold Rush. Note. 64pp. 5³⁄₁₆ x 8¼. 0-486-26472-6

CANDIDE, Voltaire. Edited by Francois-Marie Arouet. One of the world's great satires since its first publication in 1759. Witty, caustic skewering of romance, science, philosophy, religion, government — nearly all human ideals and institutions. 112pp. 5³⁄₁₆ x 8¼. 0-486-26689-3

CELEBRATED IN THEIR TIME: Photographic Portraits from the George Grantham Bain Collection, Edited by Amy Pastan. With an Introduction by Michael Carlebach. Remarkable portrait gallery features 112 rare images of Albert Einstein, Charlie Chaplin, the Wright Brothers, Henry Ford, and other luminaries from the worlds of politics, art, entertainment, and industry. 128pp. 8⅜ x 11. 0-486-46754-6

CHARIOTS FOR APOLLO: The NASA History of Manned Lunar Spacecraft to 1969, Courtney G. Brooks, James M. Grimwood, and Loyd S. Swenson, Jr. This illustrated history by a trio of experts is the definitive reference on the Apollo spacecraft and lunar modules. It traces the vehicles' design, development, and operation in space. More than 100 photographs and illustrations. 576pp. 6¾ x 9¼. 0-486-46756-2

Browse over 9,000 books at www.doverpublications.com

A CHRISTMAS CAROL, Charles Dickens. This engrossing tale relates Ebenezer Scrooge's ghostly journeys through Christmases past, present, and future and his ultimate transformation from a harsh and grasping old miser to a charitable and compassionate human being. 80pp. 5³⁄₁₆ x 8¼. 0-486-26865-9

COMMON SENSE, Thomas Paine. First published in January of 1776, this highly influential landmark document clearly and persuasively argued for American separation from Great Britain and paved the way for the Declaration of Independence. 64pp. 5³⁄₁₆ x 8¼. 0-486-29602-4

THE COMPLETE SHORT STORIES OF OSCAR WILDE, Oscar Wilde. Complete texts of "The Happy Prince and Other Tales," "A House of Pomegranates," "Lord Arthur Savile's Crime and Other Stories," "Poems in Prose," and "The Portrait of Mr. W. H." 208pp. 5³⁄₁₆ x 8¼. 0-486-45216-6

COMPLETE SONNETS, William Shakespeare. Over 150 exquisite poems deal with love, friendship, the tyranny of time, beauty's evanescence, death, and other themes in language of remarkable power, precision, and beauty. Glossary of archaic terms. 80pp. 5³⁄₁₆ x 8¼. 0-486-26686-9

THE COUNT OF MONTE CRISTO: Abridged Edition, Alexandre Dumas. Falsely accused of treason, Edmond Dantès is imprisoned in the bleak Chateau d'If. After a hair-raising escape, he launches an elaborate plot to extract a bitter revenge against those who betrayed him. 448pp. 5³⁄₁₆ x 8¼. 0-486-45643-9

CRAFTSMAN BUNGALOWS: Designs from the Pacific Northwest, Yoho & Merritt. This reprint of a rare catalog, showcasing the charming simplicity and cozy style of Craftsman bungalows, is filled with photos of completed homes, plus floor plans and estimated costs. An indispensable resource for architects, historians, and illustrators. 112pp. 10 x 7. 0-486-46875-5

CRAFTSMAN BUNGALOWS: 59 Homes from "The Craftsman," Edited by Gustav Stickley. Best and most attractive designs from Arts and Crafts Movement publication — 1903–1916 — includes sketches, photographs of homes, floor plans, descriptive text. 128pp. 8¼ x 11. 0-486-25829-7

CRIME AND PUNISHMENT, Fyodor Dostoyevsky. Translated by Constance Garnett. Supreme masterpiece tells the story of Raskolnikov, a student tormented by his own thoughts after he murders an old woman. Overwhelmed by guilt and terror, he confesses and goes to prison. 480pp. 5³⁄₁₆ x 8¼. 0-486-41587-2

THE DECLARATION OF INDEPENDENCE AND OTHER GREAT DOCUMENTS OF AMERICAN HISTORY: 1775-1865, Edited by John Grafton. Thirteen compelling and influential documents: Henry's "Give Me Liberty or Give Me Death," Declaration of Independence, The Constitution, Washington's First Inaugural Address, The Monroe Doctrine, The Emancipation Proclamation, Gettysburg Address, more. 64pp. 5³⁄₁₆ x 8¼. 0-486-41124-9

THE DESERT AND THE SOWN: Travels in Palestine and Syria, Gertrude Bell. "The female Lawrence of Arabia," Gertrude Bell wrote captivating, perceptive accounts of her travels in the Middle East. This intriguing narrative, accompanied by 160 photos, traces her 1905 sojourn in Lebanon, Syria, and Palestine. 368pp. 5⅜ x 8½. 0-486-46876-3

A DOLL'S HOUSE, Henrik Ibsen. Ibsen's best-known play displays his genius for realistic prose drama. An expression of women's rights, the play climaxes when the central character, Nora, rejects a smothering marriage and life in "a doll's house." 80pp. 5³⁄₁₆ x 8¼. 0-486-27062-9

CATALOG OF DOVER BOOKS

DOOMED SHIPS: Great Ocean Liner Disasters, William H. Miller, Jr. Nearly 200 photographs, many from private collections, highlight tales of some of the vessels whose pleasure cruises ended in catastrophe: the *Morro Castle, Normandie, Andrea Doria, Europa,* and many others. 128pp. 8⅞ x 11¼. 0-486-45366-9

THE DORÉ BIBLE ILLUSTRATIONS, Gustave Doré. Detailed plates from the Bible: the Creation scenes, Adam and Eve, horrifying visions of the Flood, the battle sequences with their monumental crowds, depictions of the life of Jesus, 241 plates in all. 241pp. 9 x 12. 0-486-23004-X

DRAWING DRAPERY FROM HEAD TO TOE, Cliff Young. Expert guidance on how to draw shirts, pants, skirts, gloves, hats, and coats on the human figure, including folds in relation to the body, pull and crush, action folds, creases, more. Over 200 drawings. 48pp. 8¼ x 11. 0-486-45591-2

DUBLINERS, James Joyce. A fine and accessible introduction to the work of one of the 20th century's most influential writers, this collection features 15 tales, including a masterpiece of the short-story genre, "The Dead." 160pp. 5³⁄₁₆ x 8¼. 0-486-26870-5

EASY-TO-MAKE POP-UPS, Joan Irvine. Illustrated by Barbara Reid. Dozens of wonderful ideas for three-dimensional paper fun — from holiday greeting cards with moving parts to a pop-up menagerie. Easy-to-follow, illustrated instructions for more than 30 projects. 299 black-and-white illustrations. 96pp. 8⅜ x 11. 0-486-44622-0

EASY-TO-MAKE STORYBOOK DOLLS: A "Novel" Approach to Cloth Dollmaking, Sherralyn St. Clair. Favorite fictional characters come alive in this unique beginner's dollmaking guide. Includes patterns for Pollyanna, Dorothy from *The Wonderful Wizard of Oz,* Mary of *The Secret Garden,* plus easy-to-follow instructions, 263 black-and-white illustrations, and an 8-page color insert. 112pp. 8¼ x 11. 0-486-47360-0

EINSTEIN'S ESSAYS IN SCIENCE, Albert Einstein. Speeches and essays in accessible, everyday language profile influential physicists such as Niels Bohr and Isaac Newton. They also explore areas of physics to which the author made major contributions. 128pp. 5 x 8. 0-486-47011-3

EL DORADO: Further Adventures of the Scarlet Pimpernel, Baroness Orczy. A popular sequel to *The Scarlet Pimpernel,* this suspenseful story recounts the Pimpernel's attempts to rescue the Dauphin from imprisonment during the French Revolution. An irresistible blend of intrigue, period detail, and vibrant characterizations. 352pp. 5³⁄₁₆ x 8¼. 0-486-44026-5

ELEGANT SMALL HOMES OF THE TWENTIES: 99 Designs from a Competition, Chicago Tribune. Nearly 100 designs for five- and six-room houses feature New England and Southern colonials, Normandy cottages, stately Italianate dwellings, and other fascinating snapshots of American domestic architecture of the 1920s. 112pp. 9 x 12. 0-486-46910-7

THE ELEMENTS OF STYLE: The Original Edition, William Strunk, Jr. This is the book that generations of writers have relied upon for timeless advice on grammar, diction, syntax, and other essentials. In concise terms, it identifies the principal requirements of proper style and common errors. 64pp. 5⅜ x 8½. 0-486-44798-7

THE ELUSIVE PIMPERNEL, Baroness Orczy. Robespierre's revolutionaries find their wicked schemes thwarted by the heroic Pimpernel — Sir Percival Blakeney. In this thrilling sequel, Chauvelin devises a plot to eliminate the Pimpernel and his wife. 272pp. 5³⁄₁₆ x 8¼. 0-486-45464-9

Browse over 9,000 books at www.doverpublications.com

AN ENCYCLOPEDIA OF BATTLES: Accounts of Over 1,560 Battles from 1479 B.C. to the Present, David Eggenberger. Essential details of every major battle in recorded history from the first battle of Megiddo in 1479 B.C. to Grenada in 1984. List of battle maps. 99 illustrations. 544pp. 6½ x 9¼. 0-486-24913-1

ENCYCLOPEDIA OF EMBROIDERY STITCHES, INCLUDING CREWEL, Marion Nichols. Precise explanations and instructions, clearly illustrated, on how to work chain, back, cross, knotted, woven stitches, and many more — 178 in all, including Cable Outline, Whipped Satin, and Eyelet Buttonhole. Over 1400 illustrations. 219pp. 8⅜ x 11¼. 0-486-22929-7

ENTER JEEVES: 15 Early Stories, P. G. Wodehouse. Splendid collection contains first 8 stories featuring Bertie Wooster, the deliciously dim aristocrat and Jeeves, his brainy, imperturbable manservant. Also, the complete Reggie Pepper (Bertie's prototype) series. 288pp. 5⅜ x 8½. 0-486-29717-9

ERIC SLOANE'S AMERICA: Paintings in Oil, Michael Wigley. With a Foreword by Mimi Sloane. Eric Sloane's evocative oils of America's landscape and material culture shimmer with immense historical and nostalgic appeal. This original hardcover collection gathers nearly a hundred of his finest paintings, with subjects ranging from New England to the American Southwest. 128pp. 10⅝ x 9.
0-486-46525-X

ETHAN FROME, Edith Wharton. Classic story of wasted lives, set against a bleak New England background. Superbly delineated characters in a hauntingly grim tale of thwarted love. Considered by many to be Wharton's masterpiece. 96pp. 5³⁄₁₆ x 8 ¼.
0-486-26690-7

THE EVERLASTING MAN, G. K. Chesterton. Chesterton's view of Christianity — as a blend of philosophy and mythology, satisfying intellect and spirit — applies to his brilliant book, which appeals to readers' heads as well as their hearts. 288pp. 5⅜ x 8½.
0-486-46036-3

THE FIELD AND FOREST HANDY BOOK, Daniel Beard. Written by a co-founder of the Boy Scouts, this appealing guide offers illustrated instructions for building kites, birdhouses, boats, igloos, and other fun projects, plus numerous helpful tips for campers. 448pp. 5³⁄₁₆ x 8¼. 0-486-46191-2

FINDING YOUR WAY WITHOUT MAP OR COMPASS, Harold Gatty. Useful, instructive manual shows would-be explorers, hikers, bikers, scouts, sailors, and survivalists how to find their way outdoors by observing animals, weather patterns, shifting sands, and other elements of nature. 288pp. 5⅜ x 8½. 0-486-40613-X

FIRST FRENCH READER: A Beginner's Dual-Language Book, Edited and Translated by Stanley Appelbaum. This anthology introduces 50 legendary writers — Voltaire, Balzac, Baudelaire, Proust, more — through passages from *The Red and the Black, Les Misérables, Madame Bovary,* and other classics. Original French text plus English translation on facing pages. 240pp. 5⅜ x 8½. 0-486-46178-5

FIRST GERMAN READER: A Beginner's Dual-Language Book, Edited by Harry Steinhauer. Specially chosen for their power to evoke German life and culture, these short, simple readings include poems, stories, essays, and anecdotes by Goethe, Hesse, Heine, Schiller, and others. 224pp. 5⅜ x 8½. 0-486-46179-3

FIRST SPANISH READER: A Beginner's Dual-Language Book, Angel Flores. Delightful stories, other material based on works of Don Juan Manuel, Luis Taboada, Ricardo Palma, other noted writers. Complete faithful English translations on facing pages. Exercises. 176pp. 5⅜ x 8½. 0-486-25810-6

FIVE ACRES AND INDEPENDENCE, Maurice G. Kains. Great back-to-the-land classic explains basics of self-sufficient farming. The one book to get. 95 illustrations. 397pp. 5⅜ x 8½. 0-486-20974-1

FLAGG'S SMALL HOUSES: Their Economic Design and Construction, 1922, Ernest Flagg. Although most famous for his skyscrapers, Flagg was also a proponent of the well-designed single-family dwelling. His classic treatise features innovations that save space, materials, and cost. 526 illustrations. 160pp. 9⅜ x 12¼. 0-486-45197-6

FLATLAND: A Romance of Many Dimensions, Edwin A. Abbott. Classic of science (and mathematical) fiction — charmingly illustrated by the author — describes the adventures of A. Square, a resident of Flatland, in Spaceland (three dimensions), Lineland (one dimension), and Pointland (no dimensions). 96pp. 5³⁄₁₆ x 8¼. 0-486-27263-X

FRANKENSTEIN, Mary Shelley. The story of Victor Frankenstein's monstrous creation and the havoc it caused has enthralled generations of readers and inspired countless writers of horror and suspense. With the author's own 1831 introduction. 176pp. 5³⁄₁₆ x 8¼. 0-486-28211-2

THE GARGOYLE BOOK: 572 Examples from Gothic Architecture, Lester Burbank Bridaham. Dispelling the conventional wisdom that French Gothic architectural flourishes were born of despair or gloom, Bridaham reveals the whimsical nature of these creations and the ingenious artisans who made them. 572 illustrations. 224pp. 8⅜ x 11. 0-486-44754-5

THE GIFT OF THE MAGI AND OTHER SHORT STORIES, O. Henry. Sixteen captivating stories by one of America's most popular storytellers. Included are such classics as "The Gift of the Magi," "The Last Leaf," and "The Ransom of Red Chief." Publisher's Note. 96pp. 5³⁄₁₆ x 8¼. 0-486-27061-0

THE GOETHE TREASURY: Selected Prose and Poetry, Johann Wolfgang von Goethe. Edited, Selected, and with an Introduction by Thomas Mann. In addition to his lyric poetry, Goethe wrote travel sketches, autobiographical studies, essays, letters, and proverbs in rhyme and prose. This collection presents outstanding examples from each genre. 368pp. 5⅜ x 8½. 0-486-44780-4

GREAT EXPECTATIONS, Charles Dickens. Orphaned Pip is apprenticed to the dirty work of the forge but dreams of becoming a gentleman — and one day finds himself in possession of "great expectations." Dickens' finest novel. 400pp. 5³⁄₁₆ x 8¼. 0-486-41586-4

GREAT WRITERS ON THE ART OF FICTION: From Mark Twain to Joyce Carol Oates, Edited by James Daley. An indispensable source of advice and inspiration, this anthology features essays by Henry James, Kate Chopin, Willa Cather, Sinclair Lewis, Jack London, Raymond Chandler, Raymond Carver, Eudora Welty, and Kurt Vonnegut, Jr. 192pp. 5⅜ x 8½. 0-486-45128-3

HAMLET, William Shakespeare. The quintessential Shakespearean tragedy, whose highly charged confrontations and anguished soliloquies probe depths of human feeling rarely sounded in any art. Reprinted from an authoritative British edition complete with illuminating footnotes. 128pp. 5³⁄₁₆ x 8¼. 0-486-27278-8

THE HAUNTED HOUSE, Charles Dickens. A Yuletide gathering in an eerie country retreat provides the backdrop for Dickens and his friends — including Elizabeth Gaskell and Wilkie Collins — who take turns spinning supernatural yarns. 144pp. 5⅜ x 8½. 0-486-46309-5

Browse over 9,000 books at www.doverpublications.com

CATALOG OF DOVER BOOKS

HEART OF DARKNESS, Joseph Conrad. Dark allegory of a journey up the Congo River and the narrator's encounter with the mysterious Mr. Kurtz. Masterly blend of adventure, character study, psychological penetration. For many, Conrad's finest, most enigmatic story. 80pp. 5³⁄₁₆ x 8¼. 0-486-26464-5

HENSON AT THE NORTH POLE, Matthew A. Henson. This thrilling memoir by the heroic African-American who was Peary's companion through two decades of Arctic exploration recounts a tale of danger, courage, and determination. "Fascinating and exciting." — *Commonweal.* 128pp. 5⅜ x 8½. 0-486-45472-X

HISTORIC COSTUMES AND HOW TO MAKE THEM, Mary Fernald and E. Shenton. Practical, informative guidebook shows how to create everything from short tunics worn by Saxon men in the fifth century to a lady's bustle dress of the late 1800s. 81 illustrations. 176pp. 5⅜ x 8½. 0-486-44906-8

THE HOUND OF THE BASKERVILLES, Arthur Conan Doyle. A deadly curse in the form of a legendary ferocious beast continues to claim its victims from the Baskerville family until Holmes and Watson intervene. Often called the best detective story ever written. 128pp. 5³⁄₁₆ x 8¼. 0-486-28214-7

THE HOUSE BEHIND THE CEDARS, Charles W. Chesnutt. Originally published in 1900, this groundbreaking novel by a distinguished African-American author recounts the drama of a brother and sister who "pass for white" during the dangerous days of Reconstruction. 208pp. 5⅜ x 8½. 0-486-46144-0

THE HUMAN FIGURE IN MOTION, Eadweard Muybridge. The 4,789 photographs in this definitive selection show the human figure — models almost all undraped — engaged in over 160 different types of action: running, climbing stairs, etc. 390pp. 7⅞ x 10⅝. 0-486-20204-6

THE IMPORTANCE OF BEING EARNEST, Oscar Wilde. Wilde's witty and buoyant comedy of manners, filled with some of literature's most famous epigrams, reprinted from an authoritative British edition. Considered Wilde's most perfect work. 64pp. 5³⁄₁₆ x 8¼. 0-486-26478-5

THE INFERNO, Dante Alighieri. Translated and with notes by Henry Wadsworth Longfellow. The first stop on Dante's famous journey from Hell to Purgatory to Paradise, this 14th-century allegorical poem blends vivid and shocking imagery with graceful lyricism. Translated by the beloved 19th-century poet, Henry Wadsworth Longfellow. 256pp. 5³⁄₁₆ x 8¼. 0-486-44288-8

JANE EYRE, Charlotte Brontë. Written in 1847, *Jane Eyre* tells the tale of an orphan girl's progress from the custody of cruel relatives to an oppressive boarding school and its culmination in a troubled career as a governess. 448pp. 5³⁄₁₆ x 8¼. 0-486-42449-9

JAPANESE WOODBLOCK FLOWER PRINTS, Tanigami Kônan. Extraordinary collection of Japanese woodblock prints by a well-known artist features 120 plates in brilliant color. Realistic images from a rare edition include daffodils, tulips, and other familiar and unusual flowers. 128pp. 11 x 8¼. 0-486-46442-3

JEWELRY MAKING AND DESIGN, Augustus F. Rose and Antonio Cirino. Professional secrets of jewelry making are revealed in a thorough, practical guide. Over 200 illustrations. 306pp. 5⅜ x 8½. 0-486-21750-7

JULIUS CAESAR, William Shakespeare. Great tragedy based on Plutarch's account of the lives of Brutus, Julius Caesar and Mark Antony. Evil plotting, ringing oratory, high tragedy with Shakespeare's incomparable insight, dramatic power. Explanatory footnotes. 96pp. 5³⁄₁₆ x 8¼. 0-486-26876-4

Browse over 9,000 books at www.doverpublications.com